MAX WEBER ON CAPITALISM, BUREAUCRACY AND RELIGION

First published in 1983

Reprinted in 2006 by
Routledge
2 Park Square, Milton Park, Abingdon, Oxon, OX14 4RN

Transferred to Digital Printing 2009

Routledge is an imprint of Taylor & Francis Group, an informa business

© 1983 Stanislav Andreski

All rights reserved. No part of this book may be reprinted or reproduced or utilized in any form or by any electronic, mechanical, or other means, now known or hereafter invented, including photocopying and recording, or in any information storage or retrieval system, without permission in writing from the publishers.

The publishers have made every effort to contact authors and copyright holders of the works reprinted in the *Weber* series. This has not been possible in every case, however, and we would welcome correspondence from those individuals or organisations we have been unable to trace.

These reprints are taken from original copies of each book. In many cases the condition of these originals is not perfect. The publisher has gone to great lengths to ensure the quality of these reprints, but wishes to point out that certain characteristics of the original copies will, of necessity, be apparent in reprints thereof.

British Library Cataloguing in Publication Data
A CIP catalogue record for this book
is available from the British Library

Max Weber on Capitalism, Bureaucracy and Religion
ISBN13: 978-0-415-40214-9 (volume)
ISBN13: 978-0-415-40210-1 (set)

Routledge Library Editions: Weber

ISBN10: 0–415–40214–X (hbk)
ISBN10: 0–415–48953–9 (pbk)

ISBN 13: 978–0–415–40214–9 (hbk)
ISBN 13: 978–0–415–48953–9 (pbk)

MAX WEBER ON CAPITALISM, BUREAUCRACY AND RELIGION

A Selection of Texts

Edited by

STANISLAV ANDRESKI

LONDON AND NEW YORK

Max Weber on Capitalism, Bureaucracy and Religion

A Selection of Texts

Edited and in part newly translated by
STANISLAV ANDRESKI
Professor of Sociology, University of Reading

LONDON AND NEW YORK

© Texts: J. C. B. Mohr, Tübingen, 1920-1.
© Translations: Stanislav Andreski; Routledge; New Left Books, 1983.
© Selection, Editorial Work and Introduction, Stanislav Andreski, 1983.
This book is copyright under the Berne Convention. No reproduction without permission. All rights reserved.

First published in 1983
by Routledge
2 Park Square, Milton Park, Abingdon, Oxon, OX14 4RN
270 Madison Ave, New York NY 10016

British Library Cataloguing in Publication Data

Weber, Max
    Max Weber on capitalism, bureaucracy and religion.
1. Weber, Max   2. Sociology
I. Title   II. Andreski, Stanislav
301'.092'4   HM22.G3W4
ISBN 0-04-301147-0
ISBN 0-04-301148-9   Pbk

Library of Congress Cataloging in Publication Data

Weber, Max, 1864-1920.
    Max Weber on capitalism, bureaucracy, and religion.
    Includes index.
    1. Capitalism.   2. Bureaucracy.   3. Religion and sociology.
    4. Protestantism and capitalism.
    I. Andreski, Stanislav.   II. Title.
HB501.W4714213   1983   330.12'2   82-22760
ISBN 0-04-301147-0
ISBN 0-04-301148-9   (pbk.)

Set in 11 on 12pt Times by Photobooks (Bristol) Ltd

Contents

Introduction by Stanislav Andreski	*page*	1
The Writings of Max Weber		13
A Note on the Sources		16

The Texts   19

1	The Uniqueness of Western Civilisation	21
2	The Failure of Capitalism in the Ancient World	30
3	The Confucianist Bureaucracy and the Germs of Capitalism in China: the City and the Guild	59
4	Hindu Religion, Caste and Bureaucratic Despotism as Factors of Economic Stagnation: the Caste and the Tribe	85
5	The Nature of Modern Capitalism	109
6	Protestantism and the Spirit of Capitalism	111
7	Religion and Other Factors in the Development of Modern Capitalism	126
8	The Distinctive Features of European Cities and the Rise of the West	138
9	The State and Business Enterprise	150
10	The End of Capitalism?	158

Index   161

Introduction

by Stanislav Andreski

As there are already three or four volumes of readings in English from Max Weber, something must be said to justify an addition to their number. The present selection differs from its predecessors in two respects. The first is that it is centred on a theme instead of presenting a cross-section of Weber's works. The theme is not arbitrarily chosen but is one which presided over Weber's studies: namely, the question of why Western civilisation developed its unique characteristics. It can be seen from the preface to his study of Protestant ethics that he more or less equated this question with the problem of the rise of capitalism, the implicit premiss being that this was the pivot on which all the other unique features of the Occident hinged. In trying to explain this process Weber attributed the chief roles to bureaucracy and religion, or rather to their interaction with the economy. For this reason I think that the texts assembled here form a more harmonious whole than can be the case with selections without a single focus, and should give the reader a good idea of how Weber explains the rise of capitalism and the civilisation associated with it.

The second distinctive feature of this selection is that it includes only texts which can be understood without a careful and laborious exegesis of their meanings, based on a wide knowledge of philosophy, history and sociological theories. Luckily this criterion to a large extent coincides with the first, because Weber is most difficult to understand when he is treating the most abstract and general questions, and much easier to follow when he analyses a concrete historic case.

A third reason for compiling this volume was that I

wished to make the texts clearer than those of most other translations. Though a great scholar and thinker, Weber was a thoroughly bad writer. Indeed, of all the great founders of the social sciences he scores the lowest for skill in presentation. In comparison with the lucidity and elegance of Adam Smith, John Stuart Mill, or de Tocqueville, Weber resembles a blunderbuss. Even within the Germanic cultural tradition – where ponderous and convoluted style was regarded as a testimonial of academic respectability – Weber seems more obscure than many other writers. Often he switches subjects in a most confusing manner. For instance, in one of the passages included in the present selection the main topic is the Chinese imperial administration. Into it is inserted a paragraph which compares it with certain arrangements in the medieval German Empire, but which is written in such a way that most readers would think that it is still the Chinese administration that he is talking about. Only with some knowledge of German historical terminology can one see that this paragraph must refer to the Holy German Empire and is inserted as a comparison. In my translation I have inserted the clarifying word where it was needed. There are many other examples of this kind of thing. However, whereas with many writers obscurity masks an emptiness of thought, with Weber it is always worthwhile forcing a way through the bush to the gold underneath. Even the parts which are not his best are worth studying carefully. He is convoluted, but never trivial or given to padding.

Some of the previous translations are acceptable but there are others which are seriously misleading. To understand an obscure writer calls for a considerable investment of effort in deciphering what he intends to say. The translation, moreover, should not be too literal, as this would make it even more difficult to understand than the original because of divergent stylistic conventions in the two languages. Especially when the aim is to make the thought of the author accessible to a wider public, the construction of the phrases must be thoroughly reorganised and the statements made more lucid. Unfortunately, it so happened that some of Weber's translators (notably Talcott Parsons) were themselves addicted to convoluted and opaque writing. When an obscure writer is translated by another obscure writer the result is obscurity to the square power, so to speak. What is even graver, the translators were often unable to solve the puzzles inherent in Weber's exposition – no doubt because their thinking in general lacked logical rigour. The result is that in many translations there are sentences and entire paragraphs which make no sense whatsoever. I pity students who are instructed to study such texts and then examined on their understanding of the incomprehensible.

The fourth aim of this book is to correct the common misunderstanding about Weber's explanation of the rise of capitalism which stems from reading the most widely known, as well as the most readable, of his works: namely, *The Protestant Ethic and the Spirit of Capitalism* (the crucial chapter of which is included here). Basing their opinion on this book alone, many people have imputed to Weber the view that Protestantism was the cause of capitalism, some of them proceeding to criticise him on that score. Although Weber never put forward this view, it must be admitted that he was not a careful writer who made sure that he was not misunderstood. Indeed, often one finds the necessary qualification in another chapter or even a different volume. Here I have tried to provide a balanced conspectus of his view as it emerges from putting together his most relevant works. Thus anyone who reads this selection will see that Weber was no doctrinaire monist who assigned supreme importance to religion and disregarded political and economic factors. As can be seen below, in his explanation of the failure of capitalism in the ancient Greek and Roman civilisations Weber assigns the leading role to the military organisation while religion is scarcely mentioned.

I may be open to the reproach that by focusing on Weber's historical explanations, while leaving out his writings on methodology and systematics, I give a very one-sided (and therefore misleading) picture of his work. The first part of my answer is that to obtain a full picture of a great thinker's work one must read everything he has written. By definition, a selection can only give a partial view; and the question is whether it is better to examine one aspect in some detail or to glance briefly at assorted samples. As the chief aim of education must be to teach people how to think, I see no value in putting together a collection of bits which seems to begin arbitrarily and lead nowhere. Reading snippets may help the reader to drop names in a drawing-room conversation but is unlikely to give him any inkling of what the author was trying to achieve. This is particularly the case with Weber because he is an untidy writer who seldom produces well-rounded formulations. Consequently, when dished out in slices cut at random, his writings become indigestible lumps which the brain cannot absorb. Unable to understand properly what Weber is saying (or trying to say), the student may learn to repeat a few profound-sounding terms but will not see the use to which they are put.

However, even if it is agreed that it is better to go deeper into one aspect of a great thinker's investigations than to glance at assorted samples of his treatment of all the questions that have attracted his attention, the present selection could be criticised on the ground that it would have been preferable to focus on Weber's methodological writings, his classification of social structures, or the definitions of concepts, rather than his historical explanations. My answer to this is, first, that there is nothing to prevent someone else from producing a selection focusing on any of these areas. Secondly, the historical analyses contained in the present volume were published in his lifetime or (in the case of those which are taken from *General Economic History*), though published posthumously, were given as lectures to undergraduates. Consequently, these writings are more flowing and less telegraphic – and have fewer unfinished sentences and endings than his abstractly comparative treatment of such topics as the classification of the structures of power.

It is important to bear in mind that Weber's most general treatment – his classificaton of social structures and forms of social interaction – was left as rough notes for a volume which he did not live to write. These notes are of great interest to a well-versed scholar as a mine of insights and suggestions, but they must not be treated as a finished product because they are too elliptical and disjointed. They are not suitable reading for a beginner or non-specialist who can only be confused by the welter of classifications and

INTRODUCTION

definitions. When Talcott Parsons rounded off these notes – which in the first German edition appear in their naked original draft – and made them into a book, he rendered the cause of learning doubtful service by leading a lot of people to approach this work in the wrong frame of mind. Even those parts of his great general treatise which Weber wrote out in full make a very heavy reading, as he jumps from example to example, often refers to an example without saying anything else about it and discusses several questions at once. All this may be comprehensible to readers who are prepared laboriously to decipher the meaning and who know enough about universal history to attach some meaning to the examples mentioned merely by name, but it can only baffle the uninitiated. Obviously, anybody who wants to have a thorough knowledge of Weber must read all his works in full (and preferably in the original as most translations contain grave mistakes). A selection ought to purvey correct (though necessarily limited) knowledge of the writer's ideas without demanding from the reader extensive previous knowledge or a vast investment of time and effort.

The historical explanations are not only easier to follow but also constitute the most valuable part of Weber's work. This applies not only to his analysis of cultural entities as wholes – that is, his volumes on China, India, and so on – but also to his cross-cultural comparative treatment of types of social structure such as feudalism or bureaucracy. Weber did not invent these concepts, and his definitions thereof are no better than those of some other writers. The weight of his contribution to the understanding of these social formations lies in what he says about how and why they underwent the actual historical transformations: why, for instance, feudalism developed in one direction in India and in another in Japan. Marvellous in their sweep, these parts of his works were left unfinished at his death, and perhaps for those reasons are very difficult to understand without a wide knowledge of universal history. For this reason I have included no extracts from these parts in the present volume, which is intended as a first introduction to Weber.

It must not be inferred from what I have just said that I

regard Weber's methodological writings as unimportant, although it is true that I regard them as less important than his historical explanations. The point about these writings is that their merit lies in raising certain questions rather than in providing adequate answers to them. It is a great achievement to have brought to light problems which have remained subjects of debates ever since, but the fact remains that Weber's own discussions of them are not the best available. On such points as ethical neutrality or methodological individualism the formulations of contemporary philosophers are clearer and less open to criticism. The chief reason for this is that philosophy of science has made great progress since Weber's time when the use of logical analysis was in its infancy. Philosophy (of the rigorously analytic kind) is a difficult pursuit, but even more difficult must be the comparative and inductive study of history aimed at formulating explanations and theoretical propositions. The baffling complexity of historical processes is the most important reason for the paucity of inductive generalisations about them; but also important seems to be the scarcity of talent and inclination needed for the task. There are many historians who love the minutiae and know an enormous range of 'facts'. On the other side there are scientists and philosophers with a talent for logical inference. Rarer seem to be people who combine the analytical and generalising bent of mind with the taste and the ability for accumulating an extensive knowledge of historical details. This may explain why Weber – who is an outstanding example of such a combination – has had few followers in the sense of people who have tried to go farther along the paths which he had opened rather than write mere commentaries on his work. The result is that Weber's historical explanations have not been superseded to the same extent as his pronouncements on the philosophy of the social sciences. This does not mean that these explanations cannot be improved upon. Far from it: on the basis of the much ampler and more precise historical knowledge available today, it ought to be possible to solve the questions which baffled Weber. Nevertheless, the fact is that many of these questions remain unanswered and Weber's work continues to provide the starting points. So, if one has no time to study the entire corpus of Weber's writings and must confine oneself to a small part of it, I have no doubt that the best choice is his historical explanations.

Weber has said so many interesting things on so many topics that a reasoned evaluation of his contribution to knowledge would greatly exceed the space available for an introduction to a book of readings where it is best to let the author speak. I have attempted to provide such an evaluation in a forthcoming book, *Max Weber's Errors and Greatness*, which can be regarded as a companion volume although it also deals with the aspects of Weber's work that are not covered in the present selection. There is, however, one point of definition which cannot be entirely by-passed: namely, the concept of rationality. As I have tried to show in the aforementioned book, Weber uses this term in many senses, some of which are indefensible. And since this term appears quite frequently in the texts included here, some advice must be given about what to make of it.

Because the word 'rationalisation' is often used roughly in the sense given to it by Freud, I must point out in passing that this is almost the opposite of what Weber is implying. In Freud's scheme 'rationalisation' means a process of inventing justifications for one's actions in which the agent himself believes but which the analyst knows to be false, having ascertained through psychoanalysis that these actions are either compulsive or serve an entirely different, unconsciously pursued goal. The classic examples are from post-hypnotic suggestion: when someone does what he has been told to do under hypnosis, and to justify these actions he gives seemingly 'rational' reasons. This is not the place to discuss the validity of Freud's theories, and I mention this only to make sure that no reader acquainted with the Freudian usage will confuse it with Weber's.

When Weber speaks of 'rationalisation of the view of the world' as a unique achievement of Western civilisation, he seems to have in mind what is more often called the rise of science and scientific outlook, or the progress of rationalism, in the sense of the belief that sense, perception and reasoning (rather than faith) are the sole or ultimate source of knowledge. When historians such as Lecky write about the rise of rationalism, this is what they mean by it. To avoid becoming confused on another score, we must bear in mind that 'rationalism' in this sense is a wider concept than what is meant by 'rationalism' in the history of philosophy, where it is contrasted with empiricism; Descartes is regarded as the founder of the former view, and Locke of the latter. In this context the question was whether ratiocination or sensation is the ultimate source of knowledge. Either option on this score is compatible with being a rationalist in the wider sense. After this warning against confusing the meanings, we can leave this philosophical chicken-or-egg question aside, as it has nothing to do with Weber's concerns.

When Weber talks about bureaucracy and industry, he speaks of 'rationalisation' in the sense not far removed from that in which it is used by business consultants, who mean thereby a process of reorganising a firm (or streamlining the organisation) in such a way that every arrangement is made to serve the general goal – in business consultancy normally assumed to be the maximisation of profit.

In many contexts – where he talks about an entire civilisation or outlook on life – we can take Weber's 'rationalisation' to mean the progress of science and the multiplication of its applications. Of course many much earlier writers (Condorcet, for example) were well aware of the importance of the progress of science, while Comte saw in it the chief source of the fundamental social and cultural transformations. Weber's claim to greatness rests not on his having discovered this trend but on his contribution towards explaining the historical causes (or rather conditions) of its unfolding.

There is another (though related) concept which can replace Weber's 'rationalisation' in other contexts. When he talks about 'rational' as opposed to 'irrational' capitalism we can infer from what he says about these formations that he has in mind a difference between the form of capitalism which develops the methods and the quantity of production, and one which does not. As we shall see later, this distinction is of prime importance and crucial to his explanation of the unique achievements of Western civilisation, but the terms

8

are just as misleading here as in other contexts. If we want a term that covers technical progress together with the growth of the quantity of production and productive equipment, we do not have to invent a neologism because this is what Marx means by 'development of the forces of production'. When capitalism promotes such development Weber calls it 'rational'. The less misleading terms 'productive' and 'industrial' are available. Although he often uses the term 'irrational' to classify the opposite form of capitalism, Weber provides also a better name for it when he speaks of 'booty' or 'political capitalism' (as the opposite of the 'rational') where money is invested in arrangements for appropriating wealth which has already been produced rather than in producing it. The Roman tax-farmers are his favourite example. The term 'political' has the advantage of being less emotive but is not very descriptive. I prefer 'parasitic' which I have used when I follow Weber's insight in trying to explain the poverty of Latin America.

When Weber talks about 'rational' authority or bureaucracy he uses this adjective in another sense still. It can be inferred from what he says about these phenomena that 'rational' can be replaced by 'formally and elaborately organised', and 'rationalisation' by 'the growth of elaborate formal organisations' or 'the process of becoming more elaborately and formally organised'. If we want a snappier word we have Spencer's expression 'advance of organisation' by which he means exactly this.

I suspect that the reason why Weber used a single term to cover so many disparate phenomena is that there is some connection between them if we look at them as conditions or aspects of the rise of industrial civilisation. This rise involved the progress of science, technology and the art of organisation which consists of cumulation of products of correct (that is, rational) reasoning. In comparison with all other civilisations, industrial civilisation based on science undoubtedly enlarged the area in which rational thinking is practised. The cumulation of the products of rational thought, however, produces unintended and often opposed effects which cannot be described as rational in any definable sense of this term. Furthermore, the products of rational thought are commonly used for opposite purposes and often in a counter-productive manner. Greater employment of rational thinking and the overall rationality of the entire social structure or culture are two distinct phenomena which do not seem to go together. Neither Weber nor anyone else has shown that they do go together, or even given any reason why we might suppose that they do. We must not, therefore, follow Weber in his rash grading of civilisations on the scale of rationality, although we can see what he may have been getting at: namely, the enlargement of the area in which rational thinking (especially calculation) is done.

Technical and economic progress required the channelling of investment into production rather than spoliation. In other words, this progress was fostered by an industrial orientation of the capitalism as opposed to the predatory or exploitive orientation of which Roman tax-farming is Weber's favourite example. For this reason, it seems, he calls industrial capitalism 'rational' and the predatory kind 'irrational', although sometimes he calls it 'political'.

To develop, industrial capitalism required an elaborate legal code regularly and predictably administered. For this reason, it seems, a legal system which exhibits these features is labelled by Weber 'rational', and a development in this direction is described as 'rationalisation of the law'.

The clustering of geniuses in time and space is often cited as evidence of their dependence on social environment, as there is no reason to suppose that the frequency of births of individuals with extraordinary abilities varies greatly in large populations. Weber's case corroborates this view: his life (1864–1920) falls squarely within the period of intellectual pre-eminence of German culture which began around the middle of the nineteenth century and ended abruptly with the assumption of power by Adolf Hitler. Weber was a near contemporary of Freud and Max Planck, while Einstein (though a good deal younger) was already recognised as a great man when Weber died. Among his contemporaries doing similar work in Germany there were at least three whose contributions to knowledge are almost

INTRODUCTION

as important as his: Karl Kautsky, Otto Hintze and Werner Sombart. Many other excellent scholars helped to win for Germany (or rather for people of German language and culture) a clear pre-eminence in social and historical studies with the exception of economic theory. Though not free from the common shortcomings of German scholarship of his time, such as ponderousness, convoluted style, needless obscurity and lack of humour, Weber fully embodies its best qualities: the tremendous dedication to the ideals of science, indefatigable industry and boldness in undertaking daunting tasks.

As an offspring of an affluent family Weber faced no great obstacles in pursuing an academic career, which in those days was very difficult for people of modest means because nobody below the rank of a professor was paid a living wage, many lecturers receiving no payment at all. In a set-up which valued highly hard work and talent Weber advanced rapidly, becoming a professor at 30. And it must be remembered that at that time this was an elevated position – much higher than that represented by the title nowadays in Germany or other countries in Europe, not to speak of America.

It is perhaps strange that, despite being civil servants, and inclined to show many traits of bureaucratic personality such as an intense preoccupation with their status, the German professors were less prone than their colleagues elsewhere to attach excessive weight to the boundaries between the disciplines. In Britain law, economics, philosophy and history were studied inside watertight compartments, with particularly deleterious effects on the writing of history, which remained very narrow. New subjects originating on the borders of older disciplines – such as social and economic history, or sociology of law – were created in Germany in Weber's lifetime. His own career illustrates the permeability of interdisciplinary borders in the German universities: he began as a lecturer in law in Berlin, then held chairs of economics at Freiburg and Heidelberg, and eventually became a professor of sociology in Vienna and Munich. His doctoral thesis on the history of the medieval trading companies, as well as his *Habilitationschrift* (a

11

thesis required for qualifying as a university teacher) on the relationship of the Roman agrarian structure with the law, cut across the division between legal and economic history. His next work – a report on the situation of the agricultural labourers in the eastern province of the German Empire – would nowadays be classified as sociological fieldwork.

Notwithstanding his extraordinary intellect, in his tastes, habits and values Weber did not diverge from the norm. He was fairly conservative and nationalist. He was also a monarchist, although he thought that Wilhelm II was a vainglorious fool. During the war he began to write articles for newspapers and take an active interest in politics, becoming a member of the German delegation negotiating the peace treaty in Versailles. It is doubtful, however, whether he could have been successful as a party politician because he did not mince his words in voicing personal opinions which were too realistic and too bluntly expressed to please the public. The most striking feature of his approach is the hard-headed and deeply probing but not cynical realism which he applied to every question he discussed.

When Weber wrote his studies, literature on the economic and social history of India was very exiguous, on China non-existent and even on the ancient Mediterranean civilisations not very abundant. Because of the scarcity of the secondary sources Weber had to work from primary sources, either translated (as in the cases of China, India and Israel) or in the original Greek, Latin and Italian. Each of his historical reconstructions would count as a respectable achievement of a lifetime. Yet he also produced his comparative studies and explanatory sketches. We shall never know what other marvels he would have produced, had he not died at the age of 56 before completing his projected volumes.

The Writings of Max Weber

1889 *Zur Geschichte der Handelsgesellschaften in Mittelalter* (On the History of Medieval Trading Companies), Stuttgart, F. Enke.

1891 *Die römische Agrargeschichte in ihrer Bedeutung für das Staats- und Privat-recht* (The Agricultural History of Rome in its Relation to Public and Private Law), Stuttgart, F. Enke.

1892 *Die Verhältnisse der Landarbeiter im ostelbischen Deutschland* (The Conditions of Rural Labour in Germany beyond the Elbe), Vol. 55 of Schriften des Vereins für Sozialpolitik, Berlin, Duncker & Humblot.

1920-1 *Gesammelte Aufsätze zur Religionssoziologie* (Collected Papers on the Sociology of Religion), 3 vols, Tübingen, J. C. B. Mohr. These appeared first as articles in *Archiv für Sozialwissenschaft* from 1906 onwards.

1921 *Gesammelte politische Schriften* (Collected Political Writings), Munich, Drei Masten Verlag. Mostly written during and just after the war.

1922 *Wirtschaft und Gesellschaft* (Economy and Society). This unfinished *magnum opus* appeared in the series of *Handbuch der Sozialoekonomik*. Some parts had appeared previously as articles, some were finished, but many end with unfinished sentences or were left as mere notes.

1924 *Gesammelte Aufsätze zur Soziologie und Sozialpolitik* (Collected Papers on Sociology and Social Policy), Tübingen, J. C. B. Mohr. Articles written between 1890 and 1914.

1924 *Gesammelte Aufsätze zur Sozial- und Wirtschaftgeschichte* (Collected Papers on Social and Economic History), Tübingen, J. C. B. Mohr. The most

important part (which takes up more than two-thirds of the volume) appeared in 1896 as an entry in the encyclopaedia of *Altertumwissenschaft*.
1924 *Wirtschaftsgeschichte*, Munich, Duncker & Humblot. English translation: *General Economic History*, ed. S. Hellman and M. Palyi, trans. Frank H. Knight, London, Collier Macmillan, 1961. Reproduced posthumously from the students' notes.

Translations into English

The Protestant Ethic and the Spirit of Capitalism (London: Allen & Unwin, 1930; New York: Charles Scribner's Sons, 1958).
From Max Weber: Essays in Sociology (New York: Oxford University Press, 1947).
Max Weber on the Methodology of the Social Sciences (Glencoe, Ill.: The Free Press, 1949).
The Theory of Social and Economic Organization (New York: Oxford University Press, 1947).
The Religion of China: Confucianism and Taoism (Glencoe, Ill.: The Free Press, 1951).
The Religion of India: The Sociology of Hinduism and Buddhism (Glencoe, Ill.: The Free Press, 1958).
Ancient Judaism (Glencoe, Ill.: The Free Press, 1952).
Max Weber on Law in Economy and Society (Cambridge, Mass.: Harvard University Press, 1954).
General Economic History (Glencoe, Ill., and London: The Free Press/Allen & Unwin, 1950).
Economy and Society, 2 vols (Glencoe, Ill.: The Free Press, 1968).
The Agrarian Sociology of Ancient Civilisations (London: New Left Books, 1979).

On Weber

There are a large number of articles and books on Weber. The best general summary of his ideas is provided in

Reinhard Bendix, *Max Weber, an Intellectual Portrait* (New York: Anchor Books, 1962).

A good account of his life and cultural background (rather than ideas) can be found in Donald G. Macrae, *Weber* (London: Fontana/Collins, 1974).

A Note on the Sources

The titles of the 'chapters' into which the texts are divided are not Weber's but mine.

Chapter 1 comes from the introduction to the first volume of *Religionssoziologie*. The first part of this volume appeared in English as a separate book, *The Protestant Ethic and the Spirit of Capitalism*. The text consists of pages 13 to 27 of this book with some omissions and some revisions of the translation.

Chapter 2 consists of pages 37 to 67 from *The Agrarian Sociology of Ancient Civilisations*. Some pages and sentences have been omitted and some revisions of the translation have been made.

Chapter 3 consists of extracts from the first volume of *Religionssoziologie*, 1920 edn. The following pages have been reproduced with substantial omissions and not always in the order in which they appear in the original: 291–305, 325–36, 346–50, 395–6, 424–8, 373–9, 385–95.

Chapter 4 consists of extracts from the second volume of *Religionssoziologie*, 1923 edn. The following pages have been reproduced with very substantial omissions and not always in the order in which they appear in the original: 1–2, 8–9, 19–20, 31–48, 67–70, 85–9, 93–8, 128–32, 102–12, 121–2.

Chapter 5 consists of pages 275–8 from *General Economic History* translated by Frank H. Knight, 1930 edn, with considerable omissions and substantial revisions of the translation.

Chapter 6 consists of pages 47–76 of *The Protestant Ethic and the Spirit of Capitalism*, with a few omissions and revisions of the translation.

Chapter 7 reproduces Chapter XXX of *General Economic History*, pages 352–69, with some omissions. The revision of the translation is extensive.

A NOTE ON THE SOURCES

Chapter 8 reproduces most of Chapter XVII of *General Economic History* with considerable revision of the translation.

Chapter 9 also consists of selections from *General Economic History*, pages 339-51, with equally thorough revision of the translation.

Chapter 10 is made up of selected passages from the closing pages of *The Agrarian Sociology of Ancient Civilisations*, pages 362-6.

The editions of Weber's works from which these selections have been made are as follows:

The Agrarian Sociology of Ancient Civilisations, trans. R. I. Frank (London: New Left Books, 1976).
Gesammelte Aufsätze zur Religionssoziologie, 3 vols (Tübingen: J. C. B. Mohr, 1920-1).
General Economic History, trans. Frank H. Knight (London: Allen & Unwin, 1930).
The Protestant Ethic and the Spirit of Capitalism, trans. Talcott Parsons (London: Allen & Unwin, 1930).

The Texts

1
The Uniqueness of Western Civilisation

A product of modern European civilisation, studying problems of universal history, is bound to ask himself to what combination of circumstances should be attributed the fact that in Western civilisation, and only there, have appeared cultural phenomena which (as we like to think) lie in a line of development having universal significance and value.

Only in the West does science exist at a stage of development which we recognise today as valid. Empirical knowledge, reflection on problems of the cosmos and of life, philosophical and theological wisdom of the most profound sort are not confined to the West, though in the case of the last the full development of a systematic theology must be credited to Christianity under the influence of Hellenism, since there were only fragments in Islam and in a few Indian sects. In short, knowledge and observation of great refinement have existed elsewhere, above all in India, China, Babylonia and Egypt. But in Babylonia and elsewhere astronomy lacked the mathematical foundation which it first received from the Greeks and which makes its development all the more astounding. Indian geometry had no method of rational proof – another product of the Greek intellect, which was also the creator of mechanics and physics. Indian natural sciences, though well developed in observation, lacked the method of experiment, which was, apart from small beginnings in Antiquity, essentially a product of the Renaissance, as was the modern laboratory. Hence medicine, especially in India, though highly developed in empirical technique, lacked a biological and particularly a biochemical foundation. A rational chemistry has been absent from all areas of culture except the West.

The highly developed historical scholarship of China did not have the method of Thucydides. Machiavelli, it is true, had predecessors in India; but all Asian political thought lacked a systematic method comparable to that of Aristotle, and was, indeed, deficient in rational concepts. Neither the anticipations in India (School of Mimamsa), nor the various extensive codifications, especially in the Near East, nor the Indian and other books of law had the strictly systematic forms of thought, so essential to a rational jurisprudence, of Roman law and of Western law under its influence. A structure like canon law is known only to the West.

A similar statement is true of art. The musical ear of other peoples has probably been even more sensitively developed than our own, certainly not less so. Polyphonic music of various kinds has been widely distributed over the globe. The co-operation of a number of instruments and also the singing of parts have existed elsewhere. All our rational tone intervals have been known and calculated. But rational harmonious music, both counterpoint and harmony; formation of the tone material on the basis of three triads with the harmonic third; our chromatics and enharmonics, not interpreted in terms of space, but (since the Renaissance) of harmony; our orchestra, with its string quartet as a nucleus, and the organisation of ensembles of wind instruments; our bass accompaniment; our system of notation, which has made possible the composition and production of modern musical works, and thus their very survival; our sonatas, symphonies, operas; and, finally, as means to all these, our fundamental instruments, the organ, piano, violin, and so on; all these things are known only in the Occident, although programme music, tone, poetry, alteration of tones and chromatics have existed in various musical traditions as means of expression.

In architecture, pointed arches have been used elsewhere as a means of decoration, in Antiquity and in Asia; presumably the combination of pointed arch and crossarched vault was not unknown in the Orient. But the rational use of the Gothic vault as a means of distributing pressure . . . and above all as the constructive principle of great monumental buildings and the foundation of a *style* extending to sculpture and painting, such as that created during our Middle Ages, does not occur elsewhere. The technical basis of our architecture came from the Orient. But the Orient lacked that solution of the problem of the dome and that type of classic rationalisation of all art – in painting by the rational utilisation of lines and spatial perspective – which the Renaissance created for us. There was printing in China. But a printed literature, designed *only* for print and only possible through it, and, above all, the press and periodicals, have appeared only in the Occident. Institutions of higher education of all possible types, even some superficially similar to our universities, or at least academies, have existed (China, Islam). But a rational, systematic and specialised pursuit of science, with trained and specialised personnel, has only existed in the West in a sense at all approaching its present dominant place in our culture. Above all this is true of the trained official, the pillar both of the modern state and of the economic life of the West. He forms a type of which there have formerly only been suggestions, which have never remotely approached its present importance for the social order. Of course the official, even the specialised official, is a very old constituent of societies. But no country and no age has ever experienced, in the same sense as the modern Occident, the absolute and complete dependence of its whole existence, of the political, technical and economic conditions of its life, on specially trained officials. The most important functions of the everyday life of society have come to be in the hands of technically, commercially and above all legally trained government officials.

Organisation of political and social groups in feudal classes has been common. But even the feudal state in the Western sense has only been known to our culture. Even more peculiar to us are parliaments of periodically elected representatives, with government by demagogues and party leaders as ministers responsible to the parliaments, although there have, of course, been parties, in the sense of organisations for exerting influence and gaining control of political power, all over the world. In fact, the state itself, in the sense of a political association with a rational, written constitution, rationally ordained law, and an administration bound to rational rules or laws, administered by trained officials, is known, in this combination of characteristics, only in the Occident, despite all other approaches to it.

The same is true of the most significant force in modern life: capitalism. The impulse to acquisition, pursuit of gain, of money, of the greatest possible amount of money, has in itself nothing to do with capitalism. This impulse exists and has existed among waiters, physicians, coachmen, artists, prostitutes, dishonest officials, soldiers, nobles, crusaders, gamblers and beggars. One may say that it has been common to all sorts and conditions of men at all times and in all countries of the world, wherever the objective possibility of it is or has been given . . . Unlimited greed for gain is not in the least identical with capitalism, and is still less its spirit. Capitalism *may* even be identical with the restraint, or at least a rational tempering, of this irrational impulse. But capitalism is identical with the pursuit of profit, and forever *renewed* profit, by means of continuous, rational, capitalistic enterprise. For it must be so: in a wholly capitalistic order of society, an individual capitalistic enterprise which did not take advantage of its opportunities for profit-making would be doomed to extinction.

Let us now define our terms somewhat more carefully than is generally done. We will define a capitalistic economic action as one which rests on the expectation of profit by the utilisation of opportunities for exchange, that is, on peaceful chances of profit. Acquisition by force is a different process.

Where capitalistic acquisition is rationally pursued, calculation underlies every single action of the partners. For the purpose of this conception all that matters is that an actual adaptation of economic action to a comparison of money income with money expenses takes place, no matter how primitive the form. Now in this sense capitalism and capitalistic enterprises, even with a considerable rationalisation of capitalistic calculation, have existed in all civilised countries of the world, so far as documents permit us to judge: in China, India, Babylonia, Egypt, Mediterranean

Antiquity and the Middle Ages, as well as in modern times. These were not merely isolated ventures, but economic enterprises which were entirely dependent on the continual renewal of capitalistic undertakings, and even continuous operations. However, trade especially was for a long time not continuous like our own, but consisted essentially of a series of individual undertakings. Only gradually did the activities of even the large merchants acquire an inner cohesion (with branch organisations, and so on). In any case, the capitalistic enterprise and the capitalistic entrepreneur, not only occasional but also regular, are very old and were very widespread.

Now, however, the Occident has developed capitalism both to a quantitative extent and in types, forms and directions which have never existed elsewhere. All over the world there have been merchants, wholesale and retail, local or engaged in foreign trade. Loans of all kinds have been made, and there have been banks with the most varied functions, at least comparable to ours of, say, the sixteenth century . . . Whenever money finances of public bodies have existed, money-lenders have appeared, as in Babylonia, Hellas, India, China and Rome. They have financed wars and piracy, contracts and building operations of all sorts. In overseas policy they have functioned as colonial entrepreneurs, as planters with slaves, or directly or indirectly forced labour, and have farmed domains, offices and, above all, taxes. They have financed party leaders in elections and mercenaries in civil wars. Their activities have been predominantly of an irrational and speculative character, or directed to acquisition by force, above all the acquisition of booty, whether directly in war or in the form of continuous fiscal exploitation of the subject populations.

The capitalism of promoters, large-scale speculators, concession hunters and, above all, the capitalism especially concerned with exploiting wars, bears this stamp even in modern Western countries, and some, but only some, parts of large-scale international trade are closely related to it, today as always.

However, in modern times the Occident has developed, in addition to this, a very different form of capitalism which has appeared nowhere else: the rational capitalistic organisation of (formally) free labour. Only embryonic forms of it are found elsewhere. Even the organisation of unfree labour reached a considerable degree of rationality only on the plantations and to a very limited extent in the slave workshops of Western Antiquity. In the manors, manorial workshops and domestic industries on estates with serf labour it was probably somewhat less developed. Moreover, developed domestic industries with free labour have definitely been proved to have existed in only a few isolated cases outside the Occident . . .

Rational, industrial organisation, attuned to regular market, rather than to political or irrationally speculative opportunities for profit, is not, however, the only peculiarity of Western capitalism. The modern rational organisation of capitalistic enterprise would not have been possible without two other important factors in its development: the separation of business from the household, which completely dominates modern economic life, and, closely connected with it, rational book-keeping . . . The development of capitalistic associations with their own accounts is also found in the Far East, the Near East and in Antiquity. But compared with the modern independence of business enterprises, those are only small beginnings. The main reason for this was that the indispensable requisites for this independence, our rational business book-keeping and our legal separation of corporate from personal property, were entirely lacking, or had only just begun to develop.

However, all these peculiarities of Western capitalism have derived their significance in the last analysis only from their association with the capitalistic organisation of labour. Even what is generally called commercialisation – the development of negotiable securities and the rationalisation of speculation, the stock exchange, and so on – is connected with it. For without the rational capitalistic organisation of labour, all this, so far as it was possible at all, would have nothing like the same significance for the social structure and all the specific problems of the modern Occident connected with it. Exact calculation – the basis of everything else – is only possible on a basis of free labour.

Just as, or rather because, the world has known no rational organisation of labour outside the modern Occident, it has known no rational socialism. True, we can find elsewhere examples of municipal control of the economy, and of food supply policy, mercantilism, welfare policies of princes, rationing, governmental regulation of economic life, protectionism and *laissez-faire* theories (as in China). The world has also known socialistic and communistic experiments of various sorts: family, religious, or military communism, state socialism (in Egypt), monopolistic cartels and consumers' organisations. But although we can find everywhere market privileges of cities, companies and guilds, and all sorts of legal differences between town and country, the concept of the citizen has not existed outside the Occident, and that of the bourgeoisie outside the modern Occident.* Similarly, the proletariat as a class could not exist, because there was no rational organisation of free labour under regular discipline. Class struggles between creditor and debtor classes, landowners and the landless, serfs or tenants, and conflicts between trading interests and consumers or landlords, have been occurring everywhere in various combinations. But even the Western medieval struggles between putters-out and their workers had only rudimentary parallels in other civilisations. The modern conflict of the large-scale industrial entrepreneur and free wage labourers has no equivalents anywhere.

In a universal history of culture the central problem for us is not ... the development of any form of capitalist activity as such: the adventurer type, or capitalism involved in trade, war, politics, or administration as sources of gain. It is rather the origin of sober bourgeois capitalism with its rational organisation of free labour. The problem is that of the cultural origins of the Western bourgeois class and of its peculiarities: a problem which is certainly closely connected with that of the origin of the capitalistic organisation of labour, but is not quite the same thing. For the bourgeois as a class existed prior to the development of the peculiar

---

* It must be remembered that 'citizen' and 'bourgeois' originally simply meant 'townsman'. (S.A.)

modern form of capitalism, though, it is true, only in Western civilisation.

The modern Western form of capitalism is dependent on science, especially the natural sciences based on mathematics and exact and rational experiment. On the other hand, the development of these sciences and of the technology resting upon them now receives important stimulus from these capitalistic interests in its practical economic applications. It is true that the origin of Western science cannot be attributed to such interests. Calculation, even with decimals, and algebra have been used in India, where the decimal system was invented. But it was only fully utilised by the developing capitalism in the West; in India it did not lead on to modern arithmetic or book-keeping. Nor was the origin of mathematics and mechanics determined by capitalistic interests. Yet the *technical* utilisation of scientific knowledge, so important for the living conditions of the mass of people, was certainly encouraged by economic considerations, which were extremely favourable to it in the Occident. But this encouragement was derived from the peculiarities of the social structure of the Occident. We must hence ask, from *what* parts of that structure was it derived, since not all of them have been of equal importance?

Among those of undoubted importance are the rational structures of law and of administration. For modern rational capitalism needs, not only the technical means of production, but also a calculable legal system and an administration based on formal rules. Without them, an irregular, shady, speculative and purely commercial capitalism as well as other kinds of politically involved capitalisms are possible, but no rational enterprise under individual initiative, with fixed capital and certainty of calculations. Such a legal system and such administration have been available as a framework for economic activity only in the Occident. We must, therefore, inquire where that law came from. Among other circumstances, capitalistic interests have in turn undoubtedly also helped, but by no means alone nor even principally, to prepare the way for the predominance in law and administration of a class of jurists specially trained in rational law. But these interests did not themselves create that law. Quite different forces were at work in this development. And why did not capitalistic interests do the same in China or India? Why did not scientific, artistic, political, or economic development there move on to that path of rationalisation which is peculiar to the Occident?

In all these matters it is a question of the specific and peculiar rationalism of Western culture. Now by this term very different things may be understood, as the following discussion will repeatedly show. There is, for example, rationalisation of mystical contemplation, that is, of an attitude which, viewed from other departments of life, is specifically irrational, just as much as there are rationalisations of economic life, of technique, of scientific research, of military training, of law and administration. Furthermore, each one of these fields may be rationalised in terms of very different ultimate values and ends, and what is rational from one point of view may well be irrational from another. Hence rationalisations of the most varied character have existed in various departments of life and in all areas of culture. To characterise their differences from the viewpoint of cultural history it is necessary to know which aspects are rationalised, and in which direction. It is hence our first concern to work out and to explain the genesis of the special peculiarity of Occidental rationalism, and of its modern form. Every such attempt at explanation must, recognising the fundamental importance of the economic factor, above all take account of economic conditions. But at the same time the opposite relationship must not be left out of consideration. For though the development of economic rationalism is partly dependent on rational technique and law, it is at the same time determined by the ability and disposition of men to adopt certain types of practical rational conduct. When these have been obstructed by spiritual obstacles, the development of rational economic conduct has also met serious inner resistance. The magical and religious forces, and the ethical ideas of duty based upon them, have in the past always been among the most important formative influences on conduct.

2
The Failure of Capitalism in the Ancient World

The pattern of settlement in the European Occident contrasts with that common among the civilisations of East Asia. The differences may be summed up briefly, if somewhat imprecisely, as follows: in Europe the transition to fixed settlement meant a change from the dominance of cattle breeding (especially for milk) to an economy dominated by agriculture, with cattle breeding continuing as a secondary element; in Asia, on the contrary, there was a shift from extensive, and hence nomadic, agriculture to horticulture without milk-cattle breeding. The contrast is relative, and may not be true of prehistoric times, but regardless of when it arose, it led to fundamental distinctions. Thus among European peoples private ownership of land is always connected with the division and final assignment of communal grazing lands among smaller groups, whereas among Asians this development did not occur and so the primitive agricultural communal units found in the West – for example, the mark* and the commons – were either unknown in Asia or else had a different economic function. For this reason the role of communal property in East Asian village organisations (unless it is of modern origin, perhaps produced by fiscal regulations) differs markedly from European parallels. Nor does one find among East Asians the 'individualism' connected with ownership of herds, with all its consequences.

Among Occidentals, therefore (mainly, but not only, in Europe), we find everywhere certain characteristics at the

---

*Pasture lands held in common by a German village.

start of development. Usually, so far as we can judge, sedentary agriculture commenced when the land available for exploitation was reduced through an increasing shift of emphasis from milk-cattle breeding to field crops. This is true not only for north-west Europe but also in essentials for south Europe and the Near East.

However, this development was profoundly modified in prehistoric times in the Near East (Mesopotamia) and in the single major African centre of civilisation, Egypt, by the fundamental importance of riverine irrigation systems. Theoretically irrigation agriculture could have evolved directly out of the later stage of horticulture which existed before the domestication of animals, but in any case irrigation gave the entire economy of these areas a very specific character in historical times.

In contrast, the Greek and also – despite the ancient sources' emphasis on the use of cattle for work, not milk – the Roman communities had agrarian systems which were fundamentally closer to those of medieval Europe. Antiquity took a different course, however, from the time when the masses, having been attached to the land for its intensive development, were no longer available for military service, so that a division of labour arose with a professional military class which then sought to exploit the defenceless masses for its own benefit. The development of military technique into a profession, presupposing permanent training and practice, sometimes accompanied this development and sometimes caused it. In the early Middle Ages of Europe this process, as we know, led to the establishment of 'feudalism'. Only the beginnings of a system similar to medieval feudalism can be found in Antiquity; there are no real analogies to the combination of vassalage and benefice or to the development of Romano-Germanic feudal law. Still, it appears unnecessary and unwise to limit the use of the concept 'feudalism' to its medieval form. Both East Asian and Amerindian civilisations had institutions which, because of their functions, we regard as essentially feudal in character. There is no reason why the concept of feudalism should not be used to characterise all those social institutions whose basis is a ruling class which is dedicated to war or royal service and is supported by privileged landholdings, rents, or the labour services of a dependent, unarmed population.*

Thus one should call feudal the administrative benefices granted in Egypt and Babylon as well as the constitution of Sparta. The differences between various forms of feudalism arise from variations in the manner in which the warrior class was organised and economically supported. One of the various possibilities is the distribution of the ruling class as landlords all over the country, as in that 'individualistic' pattern of feudalism which we find clearly delineated in medieval Europe, with origins going back to late Antiquity.

Another form, however, developed in Mediterranean and in particular Greek Antiquity, where there appeared very early 'feudal cities', fortified centres settled by professional warriors. This 'city feudalism' was not the only form of feudalism in Antiquity, but it directly influenced the later centres of 'classical' political civilisation in the beginning of their political development.

The import of a foreign and superior military technology took place in Antiquity in south Europe via the sea, and at the same time through the incorporation of conquered coastal areas into a commercial system which was, at least geographically, of considerable extent. The feudal ruling class was at first always that class which derived profit from this trade. Therefore the feudal development characteristic of Antiquity led to the formation of feudal city-states. Central Europe, on the other hand, was transformed in the early Middle Ages by a development of military technique which came to it via land routes. When central Europe was ripe for feudalism, it lacked the developed commerce such as had existed in Antiquity, and so feudalism there was based much more on the land; hence there arose the manorial system. The tie which held together the dominant military

---

* This definition would also cover centralised political formations like the Ottoman, Byzantine, or Muscovite empires, and is close to the meanings attached to this term by Marx. In his later works Weber opts for a narrower definition which entails dispersion of power as an essential characteristic, and excludes therefore the cases just mentioned as well as those with which Weber deals here. (S.A.)

class was therefore essentially that of personal allegiance, whereas in Antiquity it was the much stronger tie of municipal citizenship.

The relation between ancient city feudalism and a trade economy recalls medieval developments: the rise of free industry in the cities, the downfall of patrician rule, the latent struggle between 'city economy' and 'manorial economy', and the passing of the feudal state due to the development of money economy during the later Middle Ages and the modern epoch. However, such comparisons with medieval and modern phenomena, although seemingly quite plausible, are highly unreliable for the most part, indeed are often an obstacle to clarity and understanding. For the similarities can all too easily deceive. Ancient civilisation had specific characteristics which sharply differentiate it from medieval and modern civilisations. Its economic focus, until the beginning of the Roman Empire, was the coast in the Occident and the rivers in Egypt and the Near East. Although ancient trade, both interlocal and international, was geographically extensive and highly profitable, it nevertheless, apart from a few important interludes, lagged behind that of the later Middle Ages in the relative volume of goods traded. It is true that ancient trade was varied and included base as well as precious metals, and more numerous raw materials than one would expect. Nevertheless, ancient land trade was comparable with that of the later Middle Ages only in particular points and only in particular periods. Even in sea trade most commodities of mass consumption played a really significant role only in few periods of political or economic expansion, above all in cases where monopoly ports were established, as at Athens and later at Rhodes, Egypt and Rome.

Thus Beloch estimated that the annual trade of Piraeus in 401–400 BC was 2,000 talents (about 13 million gold francs), basing his estimate on the customs dues collected there in that year. The tariff was one-fiftieth of the value of the goods and 30 or 36 talents were collected: hence the goods were worth about 2,000 talents. Considering that this was in Piraeus alone, that it was so soon after the Peloponnesian War, that no allowance is made for changes in the purchasing power of money, and that even so 2,000 talents is approximately the equivalent of one-tenth of the foreign trade of the present kingdom of Greece* (c.130–40 million gold francs), this sum is certainly an impressive figure. It must be accepted if one assumes that in fact customs amounted to only 2 per cent of the value of goods in transit and other taxes were not included. Scholars, however, disagree on these matters.

Even more imposing is the sum of 1 million drachmae (about 140 Attic talents) which the Rhodians *claimed* their island collected in import duties before the establishment of a free port on Delos. Their island, indeed, had extraordinary privileges in virtually all Hellenistic realms, and after the establishment of Delos as a free port they only collected 150,000 drachmae. The problem here is whether we can accept this statement, the accuracy of which is somewhat doubtful owing to its obvious 'official' character. Another documented example is the 5 per cent duty collected on the maritime trade of Athenian allies, but not on the trade of Athens itself and the largest islands. This duty was collected as a substitute for certain levies, and Beloch estimates that the Athenians themselves expected it to raise 1,000 talents. I cannot accept this, however, for the passage in Thucydides on which this is based is surely too compressed to be an adequate source for determining the amount, and the figure is also irreconcilable with the 30–36 talents collected at Piraeus. Furthermore, a tribute which could be discharged by a 5 per cent increase in the price of imports seems to make no sense.

A more important business transaction, in fact probably the largest documented for Antiquity of free private trade without state control or subvention, was the flow of imports to the value of 55 million sesterces (16 million gold francs) from India to Egypt in one year under Vespasian. The evidence for this is apparently reliable.

One must bear in mind that all calculations for trade in Antiquity include not only material goods but also slaves. Because of their portability slaves were a very important

* i.e. around 1900. (S.A.)

part of commerce in times of economic expansion, and in peace they were expensive if of good quality.

In Antiquity dependence on imported grain, wherever it became a constant phenomenon, always led to state intervention and hence institutional and political consequences of fundamental importance, since private commerce was not considered adequate to ensure its provision.

Of course, not only states in the Middle Ages but also the mercantilist monarchies and even tzarist Russia had grain policies similar in purpose to those of Antiquity. However, the 'storehouse' policies of absolutist states, even that of Russia (where they were most developed), were hardly comparable in importance with those of the Babylonian and Egyptian grain storage systems, or even the Roman system of the *annona*. Furthermore, the modern absolutist states (even Russia) pursued different aims and used different methods. The element which differentiates the grain policies of ancient from modern states is essentially the contrast between the modern proletariat and the so-called ancient proletariat. The latter was a consumer proletariat, a mass of impoverished petty bourgeois, rather than, as today, a working class engaged in production. The modern proletariat as a class did not exist in Antiquity.

Ancient civilisation was either based directly on slavery or else was permeated by slavery to a degree never present in the European Middle Ages. This was partly because of the low cost of human subsistence in the centres where it flourished, partly because of historical and political conditions. Slavery was dominant in some periods, such as the later Roman Republic, and it was still a pervasive influence in other periods, such as the Hellenistic and Roman imperial ages, when legally 'free' labour prevailed. It is of course true that the documents show that in Ptolemaic and Roman Egypt an important role was played by free labour, even outside the skilled crafts. This is confirmed by the Talmud and by inscriptions. The distinctly capitalistic concept of the employer seems present in a developed form but it is characteristic that whenever there arose the need for the use of a large and reliable workforce during set periods of time, as in the Ptolemaic oil monopoly, it was necessary to impose direct or indirect limitations on freedom of movement. Indeed, slavery flourished especially in those periods and places generally associated with the zenith of 'classical' and 'free' political systems. Although I believe that prevailing views of certain areas and periods of Antiquity overemphasise the number and importance of slaves, especially for Hellenistic Egypt, but also for the earlier Near East and Greece, still the fundamental distinction between Antiquity on the one hand and medieval and modern Europe on the other remains valid . . .

There is, moreover, no evidence whatever for the existence in Antiquity of factories, even in the purely technical or operational sense of the term such as would encompass phenomena like Russia's factories manned by serfs rendering *corvée** labour or state factories producing for state needs. Nor do our sources ever indicate the widespread existence of industrial factories – that is, centres of production deserving the name 'factory' because of their size, continuity of operation and technological sophistication (involving concentration of production in workshops, division and organisation of labour and use of fixed capital).

For example: the factory was not the normal form of production even in the industries of the pharaohs, nor in the monopolies of the Ptolemies and of the later Roman Empire – periods where one would most expect to find it. The Hellenistic *ergastërion*† was simply the servants' quarters of a wealthy man, usually a merchant – often an importer of costly raw materials such as ivory. There he kept his skilled slaves – they could be of any number, and would either have been purchased or else held as collateral on loans – who worked under the directions of an overseer on that part of his raw material which he did not sell to free artisans . . . One could divide this *ergastërion* at will by selling a part of the slaves, just as one would divide an ingot of lead; this indicates clearly that we are dealing here with an undifferentiated group of slave labourers, not a differentiated organisation of labour.

* Compulsory part-time work. (S.A.)
† A large workshop. (S.A.)

Here and there 'subsidiary industries' existed to aid the market operations of large agricultural organisations, and there were workshops attached to the monopoly administrations in the Near East and under the Roman Empire. There were also textile enterprises owned by great noblewomen which undoubtedly sometimes grew to large dimensions as in medieval times. But all these concerns were dependent on plantations or tax administrations, or an *oikos*;* they were not genuine 'factories'. If one does find evidence of first steps towards something like a genuine factory organisation – and this, of course, could occur in Antiquity as it did in Russia during serfdom – it soon becomes apparent that these phenomena, like the Russian factories and for the same reasons, only serve as 'exceptions that prove the rule', for they were never a regular feature of the private sector.

Such an exception is the banking industry, which is supposed to have surpassed in size and character that of the thirteenth century quantitatively if not qualitatively. In fact, this ancient banking seems to have been in the hands of the tax farmers in a very few centres of political power, Rome in particular as well as Athens and a few others. Furthermore, different kinds of business – bottomry loans, merchant partnerships (characteristic of the discontinuity of 'early capitalism'), bank payments and transfers – were transacted with legal instruments essentially similar to those of the early Middle Ages. Thus the bill of exchange, as known in early medieval times, already existed in a rudimentary form; similarly the rates, terms and legal regulation of interest were all generally comparable to early medieval equivalents. There was, however, an absence of all forms of state debt, something which was developed in the Middle Ages, and which would have provided a regular source of return for capital. Instead there were 'substitutes' for a national debt, such as the colossal hoards of Oriental and Persian kings and Greek temples . . . All these phenomena indicate how little the existing stocks of precious metals were used as 'capital' . . .

* A self-sufficient great household and estate in ancient Greece. Weber applies this term also to similar formations elsewhere. (S.A.)

Antiquity knew not only the unfree and half-free but also the free peasant, as owner or tenant or share-cropper. Likewise there existed, side by side with cottage industry and slave labour shops, production by free artisans – some working on order, some for wages (this was much more common) and some as extra help (this also was common). There were family workshops, one-man shops (much the most frequent) and shops run by a master with one or more slaves and free or (usually) unfree apprentices. There also existed joint co-operatives of artisans similar to the Russian artel, as well as organised teams of skilled craftsmen brought together by a contractor for a specific purpose.

Nevertheless, Antiquity had no word corresponding to our 'journeyman', a concept which arose out of the medieval struggle against the 'masters', another notion unknown to Antiquity. For throughout Antiquity, despite its wealth of civic associations, the crafts never reached that level of autonomous organisation which was attained by the high Middle Ages, nor did they reach medieval levels of refined division and organisation of labour.

Where one finds a guild or something similar in Antiquity it is nearly always essentially a state organisation for the forced imposition of public tasks. The social position of the artisan was very low, with ephemeral and partial exceptions in the Hellenic democracies, and these exceptions are apparent rather than real. But even the employers evidently never had sufficient political power to secure legal concentration of trade in the cities, such as was achieved in the Middle Ages.

Finally, Antiquity knew the free, unskilled wage earner; this type developed gradually from individuals sold into temporary slavery by themselves or by others. Wage earners were hired for harvesting, and were used by the state in large numbers for excavation work, construction and other public projects. Otherwise their employment was generally scattered and irregular.

The question to be considered now, therefore, is: did a capitalist economy exist in Antiquity, to a degree significant for cultural history? To begin with, there is a general factor: the economic surplus of the ancient city – and this applies to the Near East as well as to the archaic *polis* of the Mediterranean lands – always had its original basis in the rents which the landed princes and noble clans derived from their estates and from levies on their subjects. This was true to a degree unknown today except in the case of certain capitals centring on a royal court; an appropriate comparison would be Moscow during the period of serfdom. This source of wealth and the political situation connected with it remained throughout all Antiquity very important for the economic 'flowering' of the cities – and also for their swift decline. The ancient cities were always much more centres of consumption than production, whereas the opposite is true of medieval cities.

In the light of these factors one must then ask: although there were periods of Antiquity marked by a dramatic rise and fall in wealth, were these developments really part of an economic structure which we can call 'capitalist'?

Our answer will depend on our definition of 'capitalist' – and that, of course, can take many forms. However, one element must be emphasised: capital always means wealth used to gain profit in commerce. Otherwise the term loses any classificatory use. Therefore we should expect a capitalist economy to be based on commerce. This means that goods are produced (in part, at least) to become objects of trade, and also that the means of production are themselves objects of exchange. This excludes all manorial charges levied in rural areas on subject groups, like the various tributes – rents, dues and services – exacted from peasants in the early Middle Ages, who had to pay dues in kind and money on their possessions, inheritances, trade and persons. For neither the land owned nor the people subjected can be regarded as 'capital'; title to both depended (in principle) not on purchase in the open market but on traditional ties.

Analysis of domain agriculture is difficult because one finds a great variety of gradations; they range from systems based on formally free transfer and lease of land to *coloni** on a market basis, to systems based on completely traditional

---

* Dependent cultivators. (S.A.)

social ties binding the lord and the cultivator owing him labour services to reciprocal obligations. Nevertheless, the latter is by far the more common type wherever the land is worked by a colonate. In such cases the *coloni* are not themselves 'capital', for they are not part of an autonomous labour market, but their labour along with the land they work can become objects of trade, and in fact became such in the Near East and later Roman Empire. In these cases the system is intermediate in character: it is capitalist in so far as goods are produced for the market and the land is an object of trade; it is non-capitalist in so far as the labour force as a means of production cannot be bought or leased in the open market.

Slave agriculture, when the slaves are normal objects of trade (it makes no difference whether particular labourers have been actually purchased or not), and the land worked is privately owned or leased, is of course capitalist in character from the economic point of view. That is because land and slaves are both acquired in the open market and are clearly 'capital'. The workforce is bought, not hired as in enterprises conducted with free labour; or if labour is, exceptionally, hired, it is not from the slave but rather from his owner. Hence the capital needed for slave labour is significantly more than would be needed – other things being equal – for the same quantity of free labour. Similarly, buying land demands commitment of more capital than would leasing it.

Finally there is the large-scale capitalist enterprise based on 'free' labour . . . In general this form of enterprise was not a regular feature of private economic activity in Antiquity, either in agriculture or outside it. Large enterprises which were on a regular basis and used only hired (that is, free) labour existed in certain state undertakings, but private enterprises of this sort did not play a significant role in the social or economic systems of the centres of classical culture. This does not apply entirely, however, to the later period of the Near East.

It has been argued that capitalist economy did not play a dominant role in Antiquity, and did not in fact exist. However, to accept this view is to limit needlessly the concept of capitalist economy to a single form of valorisation

THE FAILURE OF CAPITALISM IN THE ANCIENT WORLD

of capital – the exploitation of other people's labour on a contractual basis – and thus to introduce social factors. Instead we should take into account only economic factors. Where we find that property is an object of trade and is utilised by individuals for profit-making enterprise in a market economy, there we have capitalism. If this is accepted, then it becomes perfectly clear that capitalism shaped whole periods of Antiquity, and indeed precisely those periods we call 'golden ages'.

We must avoid exaggeration, however. In particular, it is necessary to show the specific peculiarities of the various types of capital goods, and the manner of their valorisation, which determined the course of ancient economic history. Among the types of capital goods that we do not find, of course, are all those tools of production which were devised during the last two centuries of technological advance, and which today constitute what we call fixed capital. On the other hand Antiquity had a form of capital goods now in disuse: debt or chattel slaves. Similarly, among the forms of capitalist enterprise in Antiquity a very small role was played by the workshop and an even smaller one by the factory. On the other hand a form of economic activity now of little significance was of absolutely dominant importance in Antiquity: government contract.*

The most important forms of capital investment in Antiquity were as follows: (1) government contracts for partial or total collection of taxes and public works; (2) mines; (3) sea trade, with ownership of ships or part-ownership, especially through bottomry loans; (4) plantations; (5) banking and related activities; (6) mortgages; (7) overland trade. The last only sporadically became a regular, large-scale enterprise – in the West only during the first two centuries of the Roman Empire and only with respect to trade with the north and north-east; most overland trade was in goods sent on consignment by caravan. Also important were: (8) leasing out slaves (sometimes educated slaves) or establishing slaves as independent artisans or merchants in return for a percentage of income (or *obrok*, as

---

* 'Now' means here the last decades of the last century. (S.A.)

the Russians would say); (9) finally, capitalist exploitation of slaves skilled in a craft, either owned or leased, sometimes in a workshop and sometimes not.

That slaves were frequently used in private economic enterprises cannot be doubted. Artisans were to be seen working alongside a few slaves of their own. Although there is no proof of its existence in the classical period proper, we can certainly assume that there existed the 'domestic system', in which the master provides raw materials and tools, and the slave makes up the finished product in his own family household and then delivers it to the master. Certainly this existed in the Near East, and it was dominant in ancient Egypt. We may, therefore, assume such a system in the Athenian pottery industry, even though many exports bear the same name (so far the largest group numbers about eighty). The name is, of course, that of an artist, not that of a 'manufacturer' or 'contractor'. The artist's name will have been that of a family of potters in which technical skill was passed on as an inheritance and as a secret, and the name would be kept as an eponym. In this connection we should note the existence of artisans' villages in Attica, characteristic of the family-like organisation of handicrafts.

The quantitative and also the qualitative importance of capitalist enterprise in Antiquity were determined by a number of independent variables which appeared in very different combinations at different times. These variables were as follows:

1 It is clear that the supply of precious metals had great importance for the rate of capitalist development. However, there is now a mistaken tendency to overestimate the importance of this factor for the structure of the economy as a whole. Thus Babylonia had no mines and evidently very little precious metal, as is indicated by the correspondence between Babylonia's kings and the Egyptian pharaohs, and also by the use of precious metals only as a measure of value; nevertheless, from earliest times Babylonia's exchange system was as developed as that of any other Eastern land, and more developed than that of gold-rich Egypt. Similarly, capitalism was not particularly important as a basic element

of the economic structure of Ptolemaic Egypt, even though the Ptolemies had colossal hoards of precious metals (taking current estimates as at least approximately correct) and their economy was thoroughly monetarised. In fact capitalism developed to a greater extent in contemporary Rome.

There is also the strange theory that the transition to non-monetary economy in the later Roman Empire was the result of a fall in the productivity of the mines. This probably reverses the actual sequence of cause and effect; where a decline in mining productivity did occur, it was most likely caused by a shift from the classical period's mining system, based on a highly developed capitalist organisation using slave labour, to a new system based on small contractors.

The foregoing, however, should not be taken as a denial of the significance of control over large supplies of precious metals and in particular the important effects for cultural history of the sudden appearance of such supplies. Some examples: (*a*) ancient kingship usually depended on the royal treasure; (*b*) without the mines of Laureion there would probably have been no Athenian fleet; (*c*) the transfer of many temple treasuries into the circulating money supply during the Hellenic period probably had much to do with price changes *c*.500 BC; (*d*) the release of the Achaemenids' hoard furthered Hellenistic city foundations; (*e*) the effects on Rome of the colossal influx of precious metals won as war booty in the second century BC are well known. However, the fact that this booty was used as it was and not otherwise – for example, it was not hoarded, as in the Near East – must have been due to the prior existence of certain conditions. In other periods of Antiquity the presence of large stores of precious metals failed to have a 'creative' significance; that is, they did not promote the development of qualitatively new forms of economic activity.

2   The economic specificity of the capitalist use of slave labour, in comparison with free labour systems, is that a much greater amount of capital must be invested to assemble and maintain the workforce. When low sales cause suspension of production not only does the capital invested in slaves bring no interest – as is true of capital invested in

machines – but the slaves literally 'eat up' more and more of it. The result is to slow down capital turnover and capital formation.

Furthermore there was a large risk in investing capital in slave labour. This was due first of all to the fact that slave mortality was very high and entirely unpredictable, causing capital loss to the owner. Furthermore, any political upheaval could wipe out completely investments in slaves. This is reflected in the dramatic variations in slave prices; thus Lucullus sold prisoners into slavery at 4 drachmae apiece at a time when the regular market price, due to low supply, had risen to several hundred drachmae for an able-bodied labourer. The result of this was that capital invested in slaves could be drastically devalued at any time.

Moreover, there was no basis for reliable cost accounting, the necessary condition for large industrial enterprises based on division of labour. Along with this there was also the fact that patriarchal slavery, in the form prevalent in the Near East, either made the slave a member of the master's household or else conceded to him the right to have his own family household. In the latter case there could of course be no question of gaining maximum return on investments; the slave either paid dues, thus functioning as a source of rents rather than labour, or else performed work, possibly with his family, in which case he filled the role of serf or unfree houseworker with all the limitations on profit-making this implied.

Another limitation on the truly capitalist exploitation of slaves as a means of production was the fact that the slave market depended for supply on successful wars. Full capitalist exploitation of the workforce was possible only if the slaves had no families, in fact as well as in law; in other words, if they were kept in barracks, which, however, made reproduction of slaves impossible. For the cost of maintaining women and rearing children would have been a dead weight on the working capital. Sometimes this could be recovered by putting women to work in textile production, but there were difficulties here due to the peculiarities of the consumption pattern and the importance of domestic spinning and weaving in Antiquity. As for the children, there is evidence in a passage of Appian (*Civil Wars*, I.1.7) that at least during certain periods of Roman history slaves were bred on a massive scale for profit, as was done in the southern states of the USA, thus supplying slave capital in part for production and in part for replenishment. However, this interpretation of the evidence remains open to question; the precipitous price fluctuations in the slave market must have made slave-rearing very risky.

Furthermore, female labour was not suited for the major slave labour industries – plantations, seafaring, mining and tax farming. Hence it was a general rule that profit-making enterprises relied mainly on male slaves when it was possible, that is, when warfare provided the market with a stable supply of them; indeed, there is no evidence of females as farm labourers in the time of Cato or as workers in Athenian *ergastëria*. In such periods, female slaves were used for prostitution or housework. If, however, the market ceased to receive regular supplies over a period of any length, then the slave force had to be replenished through natural increase, which led to the abolition of slave barracks and the establishment of slave family households. The slaves then became themselves responsible for the replacement of slave capital, and this imposed limitations on exploitation of the workforce. Slaves could no longer be worked in chains and whipped in a plantation system; the result was inevitably to decrease profits, except where a way was found to use the economic self-interest of slaves for the benefit of their masters.

Not only was slave capital insecure and subject to unpredictable risks, there was also the fact that the slaves used in large enterprises naturally had no interest in any technical advance or any increase in the quantity or quality of production. The moral qualities which render slaves amenable to exploitation are precisely those which make them most inefficient as workers in a large enterprise. Therefore, besides attrition of slave capital there was also attrition of capital invested in draught cattle and work tools. There was also stagnation in technology; for example, there was no improvement in the plough.

Indeed, large-scale use of slave labour was in general

really profitable only when the land was fertile and the market price of slaves was low. Hence slave labour was normally used for extensive agriculture.

For these reasons, there was no regular use of skilled slave labour in large-scale enterprises based on division of labour. Isolated cases are found, but always on a small scale. Even the *ergastërion*, essentially an agglomeration of independent workers, found mainly in thriving economic centres like Athens, Rhodes and Alexandria, developed always as an annex to a trading firm or rentier household. Great households of princes and noblemen often had more dependent labour or unfree house labour than they needed, or an excess supply of goods from their domestic production, and these surpluses then appeared on the market; but one must be careful not to confuse this phenomenon with the existence of 'factories' based on purchased slaves.

There were also half-capitalist formations, based on the use of forced labour to establish 'subsidiary enterprises' within the establishments of monarchs and great slave-owners, and similar to many 'factories' in the Russia of 1700–1830. But these could exist only as monopolies, and only under certain conditions, among them being cheap food, monopoly prices for the products and low slave prices. The rate of profit also had to be high enough (30–100 per cent in Demosthenes and Aeschines) to cover the risks of slave mortality, for it to be economically possible to use purchased slaves in the master's workshop on a regular basis. Even then, however, these enterprises had no more than a few dozen workers at most. Nor did they have the fixed capital which is characteristic of a factory. Loans were made on the slaves as collateral, but not on the workshop. The slaves in fact constituted the workshop or plant, and their maintenance by the master was the crucial factor, not their employment in a single production unit. The workshop, on the other hand, was a part of the great household, and hence there is no trace in Antiquity of all those fundamental legal developments which as early as the thirteenth and fourteenth centuries – long before the appearance of modern factories – accompanied the separation of family household from workshop in medieval Europe and of private from business property. Hence, too, with a few exceptions, there was no development of business organisations like our joint stock company which could ensure continuance of enterprises despite the uncertainties which accompany partnerships; the exceptions, as one might expect, occurred in tax farming.

Similarly, the use of large numbers of slaves on an industrial scale in mines and quarries and on public works was almost entirely a matter of exploiting unskilled labour. Unfree domestic labour was a type of corvée, and was subject to the usual economic disadvantages. It is therefore doubtful how much use for it was found in production for the market. Pharaohs and priests used house labour mainly to supply the needs of temple, court and state, especially of course if the raw material was imported or mined by the temple itself or the pharaoh. Some of the product may, however, have been marketed on the side. In any case, unfree domestic labour, wherever it appeared, meant work within the slave's own small family household. Skilled slave labour was only used regularly in large industrial enterprises (save for the few large centres of commerce) in managerial positions. Thus slaves served as foremen and inspectors in mines and on plantations, and as cashiers and accountants (since they were subject to interrogation under torture) in offices, and the like. Men in these positions formed a kind of slave aristocracy, and they enjoyed the right to their own (quasi-) family and their own (quasi-) property; sometimes they were even allowed the right to dispose of their property by will (as with Pliny's slaves), and also – most important – were generally given the chance to purchase their freedom. All this was, of course, in the interest of their masters.

Skilled slaves, both those trained before enslavement by war or bankruptcy and those trained at their masters' expense merely as a source of rents, were often leased out in large numbers as 'wage earners', with the lessee bearing the risks of slave mortality. Or else a skilled slave was set up in his own shop as an independent artisan or tradesman. This was yet more profitable, since it enlisted the slave's own self-interest. The master received a regular income and could increase it up to the point where the slave's self-interest was discouraged. He could also allow the slave to amortise his own capital value, which was essentially what was involved in letting the slave use his earnings to buy his own freedom. In such cases, furthermore, the master reserved for himself certain levies and services after manumission, and also appropriated a portion of the freedman's estate at his death, sometimes all of it. The portion taken was fixed by law or contract or will; Roman law was especially rich in alternatives here.

The risk of capital loss caused by death was lessened once the slave established his own business and family and trained his children. Slave law generally made the master liable for his slave's business debts only up to the amount of the slave's own property, which of course the master was legally entitled to appropriate. That this power was not unduly abused in Antiquity, at least by the *large* slave-owner, was probably due to the necessity of encouraging the slave's economic self-involvement, and also to the skill with which slaves concealed their wealth; both were also significant factors in Russia before the emancipation of the serfs.

Manumission was common in all periods of Antiquity, at times so common that legal regulation was necessary. Naturally it was never due primarily to vanity or to the desire to enlarge a political clientele; rather, its importance indicates how effective was the slave's economic self-interest. Manumission, in fact, provided a more secure way of realising profit from slave ownership. Its economic effect, however, was to transform the capitalist exploitation of the slave as a means of production into the acquisition of profit from the slave as a source of rent and manumission money.

Hence 'the struggle between free and unfree labour' took place in the sphere of small business, both craft and trade. It was not a struggle between large-scale slave enterprise and small-scale free artisanal enterprise.

The free but propertyless groups in Antiquity included peasants, tenants, hawkers and wage earners. Alongside them there were two other groups: (1) a class of free, small property owners, engaged in trading and in small-scale production on order; often they were assisted in field or workshop by one or a few slave 'fellow workers', won as war booty or bought with savings; (2) a class of unfree skilled craftsmen, shopkeepers, serfs and tenant farmers.

Members of the latter group functioned as unfree but economically autonomous agents. They stood in much the same relation to their masters as that between free peasants, shopkeepers, or artisans and their creditors, or that between free share-croppers and their landlords. In other words, the master was simply a recipient of tribute, and the slave was exploited as a source of rents. In order to realise profit for the masters this system obviously demanded an extensive division of labour within a local money economy. Once these conditions were satisfied this system was able to maintain itself in competition with the use of slaves as means of production, and even as a rule to expand. That was especially true when the masters were much involved in politics and could not direct their business affairs personally; for example, full citizens of the *polis* as opposed to metics* in Greece and members of the senatorial nobility as opposed to equestrians in Rome. Another condition propitious for this development was a continuously high price level in the slave market.

As for competition between free and unfree labour, tenant farming was in Antiquity, as at present, the most remunerative way to exploit landed property, where there was high population density and high land prices, and consequently an emphasis on intensive agriculture, with freedom of movement and absence of relationship of bondage. Small farming was certainly dominant in ancient agriculture, slave labour being used in general on plantations, including those devoted to oil and wine production. Grain cultivation, given the technology of Antiquity, demanded too much individual effort to allow the normal use of slave labour. Indeed, the use of slave labour on a large scale was only profitable in agriculture at times when slaves were cheap and plantation products at the same time commanded high prices.

In trade and handicrafts, however, the opportunity for slaves to buy their freedom generally served as an effective spur, even more so when the privilege of keeping savings was

* Free permanent inhabitants of foreign origin or descent. (S.A.)

also conceded. It was no accident that freedmen prospered, for they had acquired habits of industry and thrift while slaves. Their success was also due, of course, to their exclusion from politics.

Inscriptions dating from the Roman Empire indicate that slave labour was less important in the Near East than in the West, even in handicrafts; and that slaves were used in the main for heavy, unskilled work. The first phenomenon was partly the result of prior economic patterns inherited from the past but it was also a result of the fact that the Roman (that is, Western) slave market had, for political reasons, a better supply. The second phenomenon was simply a consequence of the natural reluctance of masters to accept the risks and expense involved in putting slaves through a long apprenticeship.

Consequently one should not think of the effects of slave labour as simply – or even mainly – a matter of driving out free labour. Rather, its main effect was to discredit work because so much of it was done by foreign slaves bought in the market; there was, however, a general tendency to drive out free labour wherever armies were not recruited (as in the Hellenistic Near East) from professional soldiers, mercenaries, or alien ruling peoples. When wars were bitter and constant, when victory inclined now to one side and then to another, and when this kept the free population away on campaigns for years at a time, then the inevitable result – as Appian reports – was to favour slave labour as opposed to free labour, and indeed every form of slave exploitation.

On the other hand military expansion and great victories typically led to an increase in the slave supply and a reduction in slave prices, and hence furthered the capitalistic exploitation of slaves in private enterprises – plantations, navigation, mining, handicrafts, and so on. In agriculture capitalist exploitation of slave labour was profitable when another variable was present – cheap land. This occurred irregularly as the result of military expansion or revolutionary confiscation, regularly where a small population was settled on a large area of fruitful land alongside developing municipal centres of consumption. The latter situation obtained in Rome after the unification of Italy and Rome's first overseas conquests, to a degree indeed never matched either before or after. This, and similar considerations discussed above, bring us to a third problem: the influence of politics.

3   In each country political developments and conditions shaped the relative growth of free and unfree labour, and also the degree and manner in which unfree labour was subjected to capitalist exploitation. L. M. Hartmann has demonstrated the importance of military burdens imposed on free populations, and has shown that it furthered use of slave labour most of all where levies recruited from the tenants and small landowners had to equip themselves and fight a series of major wars. Well-known examples of this occurred during the flowering of Greek democracy and in the Roman Republic. Conditions were just the opposite when the army, or at least part of it, was a feudal levy, or was an autocrat's professional or mercenary or serf army; these types existed in Egypt, many Hellenistic states, the late Greek *polis* and the later Roman Empire. From the variety of economic systems in the last group of states it is apparent that military organisation by itself determined neither the degree to which slavery developed, nor consequently the degree or direction in which capitalism developed. On the other hand, economic life was always much affected by the political systems of Antiquity; in particular by the type of administration which arose from the constitution in question. Most important of all in this respect was the financial administration.

4   The organisations of public finance were the oldest large-scale enterprises of Antiquity, and they remained the largest. They developed gradually out of the great households of the city princes with their hoards of precious metals. In part these enterprises functioned as substitutes for private capital accumulation, in part they were pacemakers for it and in part they throttled it. Let us examine each aspect.

(*a*)   Finance authorities were substitutes for private capital most clearly in the bureaucratically directed compulsory labour systems of pharaonic Egypt, which originally had no private entrepreneurs. The financing of the large public projects of the Greek cities, which were let to private contractors (as the inscriptions show), was also arranged by advances of working capital from the state treasury, which indicates that there were no private accumulations of capital sufficient to finance such large projects, so that monies raised as tribute by political or religious authority had to fill the gap. In such cases the entrepreneur was essentially hired for a fee to organise the necessary clerical and labour force, as the cities – unlike the pharaonic administration – did not have the bureaucracy necessary to oversee building and had no pool of compulsory labour supply, since citizens had been freed from labour dues and the city slaves were fully employed in government offices, registries, the treasury, the mint and sometimes in building roads.

As for tax farming, it should be remembered that in many cases precisely that feature was absent which we are accustomed to think of as characteristic of the role of private capital: payment in advance. Often the tax farmers deposited their guaranteed payments only after they had collected all, or more often an agreed part, of the taxes. When the state possessed an executive officialdom, such as appears in the revenue laws of Ptolemaic Egypt, then tax farmers did not even collect taxes; the state did so, and the tax farmers either made up any deficit that appeared after converting taxes in kind into money, or else profited if there was a surplus. Here the purpose of farming the taxes was evidently no more than to obtain a secure cash basis for the state budget by insuring a minimum income in currency.

It was a new aspect of the development of tax farming in Hellenistic terms that tax farmers did in fact often have the obligation of making at least partial advance payments. Nevertheless the sums paid, though often high, do not allow us to infer the existence of correspondingly large capital accumulations. However, the system of state contracts, especially in the area of tax farming, was clearly an important factor in capital formation and, indeed, in Greece one of the most important.

(b) Public finance could function as a mere pacemaker for private capital formation only in city-states which had no bureaucratic apparatus and, instead, used state contractors to administer conquered territories and domains as well as to collect tributes from enormous areas. In Antiquity this was the case in Republican Rome, in which there developed a powerful class of private capitalists, undoubtedly based from the beginning on the state contract system. In the era of the Second Punic War – the time is significant – they supported the state with money in the manner of modern banks, and in return were able to determine the state's policies even during the war. Their thirst for profit was such that a reformer like Gracchus had to give them control of provinces and courts in order to win them over, and their struggle with the senatorial aristocracy (whom they controlled economically as money-lenders) dominated the last century of the Republic. Ancient capitalism reached its high point in this period, as a consequence of these circumstances and of the unique political structure of the Roman state.

(c) On the other hand, the organisation of public finances of the ancient states stifled the development of private capitalism in various ways. Above all, the general political basis of ancient states typically reinforced the great instability of capital formation and investment inherent in the ancient economies. There were many pressures working in the same direction. Among them were the levies in money, kind, or service imposed on the propertied classes, and the unrestrained use of the sovereign power of the Greek city-states – especially in the democracies – over the private property of their citizens; in late Hellenistic terms, a city's loans were still sometimes secured by mortgaging all its private real estate, a practice unknown in the Middle Ages. Furthermore, there was the danger of confiscations, which occurred at every political upheaval and change in the position of parties in ancient communities; as well as the not uncommon and wholly arbitrary expropriations by monarchs, such as the seizure of 'half of Africa' by Nero.

However, much more important than these catastrophes, which affected only particular interests or communities, was the general limitation imposed by public administrations on the profits of private capital, and thereby on capital formation. This limitation varied significantly. It was much more pronounced in the ancient monarchies than in the republics. The ancient monarch and members of his court were always great agrarian lords, whose position was secured partly in private law, partly in arbitrary domination exercised over conquered populations forced to pay tribute and denied any legal title to their land. The ancient city-states could also control such possessions, and indeed the Roman Republic did so on a colossal scale.

Where a city-state had such possessions, they were primarily objects of purely economic exploitation by the changing cliques surrounding prominent political leaders – above all their financiers. Consequently, city-states, especially Rome, subjected their possessions to brutal exploitation by private capital through usurious tax farming, rent squeeze combined with usury and slave trading. A monarch, however, had to act otherwise. In the first place he regarded the inhabitants of his domains essentially in more political terms – that is, as props of his dynasty. Furthermore, a monarch naturally tended, in his own interest, to value security of revenues much more highly than would a republican government directed by officials elected for short terms; for the latter and their followers, immediate profit was much more important. Hence a monarch's financial policy would be oriented more towards the political and economic interests of the state and hence would aim at a prudent and durable rate of exploitation based on the actual resources and capacity of his subjects. City-states, on the contrary, looted subject populations for the benefit of capitalist interests. Thus royal domains were generally let to small tenants, and the use of large contractors and slave plantations was very much the exception. It is true that the Roman emperors preferred large tenants on their family estates for pecuniary reasons, but on state domains they followed the normal rule.

The crux was tax farming, the most important form of capital investment in Antiquity. In Republican communities it was so central that it always tended to make the state into an enterprise based on tax loans and tax contracts, like medieval Genoa. In monarchical states, on the contrary, tax farming was always held in check, often entirely or nearly entirely under state control, and always restricted in its profits. This, of course, reduced its role in capital formation. This process of control, monopoly and bureaucratic regulation – often leading to the complete exclusion of private capital – developed inexorably in all the great monarchies of Antiquity. Gradually it transformed the administration of taxes and domains, and also the supervision of the mines and of politically important activities such as the grain supply and the delivery of provisions for the court, army and public works. Furthermore, it led to the emergence of state and municipal banks enjoying monopoly status, which handled all money-changing in the Hellenistic monarchies and municipalities.

Thus there was a sharp distinction between the city-states and monarchies of Antiquity. In the city-states there always remained the possibility of accumulating and investing capital although the character of their constitutions greatly heightened the insecurity of capital, less because of repeated efforts to attain economic equality among the citizenry – efforts which were nearly always unsuccessful – than because party conflict and warfare constantly led to political and economic catastrophes of every sort.

In the monarchies, on the other hand, capitalism was gradually checked by bureaucratic regulation. Large private accumulation in particular fared badly, for its major sources of profit were blocked, and so it was slowly starved out . . . exploitation of rural areas by cities, as primordial in Antiquity as in the Middle Ages, came to a halt, and expansion through conquest of new lands and populations stopped. The supply of cheap slaves and exploitable land, essential for growth in a capitalist slave labour economy, ceased to be plentiful and eventually dried up.

Stagnation and decline in capital formation were regularly accompanied by measures designed to ensure provision for the needs of the state. This process, well described recently by Rostovtzeff, meant a steady increase in and differentiation of the number of those made liable with their persons or property for the performance of tasks assigned by the authorities. Such persons were tied to their land and social function by administrative law, until eventually society was universally dominated by a system of obligatory services, which abolished all that men of the 'classical' periods called freedom, in a mutation typical of the so-called 'decline' of ancient states.

Thus monarchical regulation, though beneficial to the great mass of subjects, spelt in fact the end of capitalist development and everything dependent on it. Slavery as a basis of capitalist enterprise regressed and new capital formation ceased, because the profit margin allowed had sunk below the indispensable minimum needed by ancient capital. Instead the economy became dominated by labour which was formally 'free', but was in fact subject to administrative law and direction. Wherever, in addition, the monarchy assumed a theocratic character, there we always find that religion and law sanction 'protection of the weak' as in the Near East, and this set rather precise limits to capitalist exploitation of men.

For agrarian history the results of this development were always the same. The relative importance of slave plantations declined while small tenant farming – especially share-cropping – became the main form of land use. Estates exploited for rents by princes, and landowners holding their land from princes on a semi-private basis, became the predominant category of property in the countryside.

To sum up, the most important hindrance to the development of capitalism in Antiquity arose from the political and economic characteristics of ancient society. The latter, to recapitulate, included: (1) the limits on market production imposed by the narrow bounds within which land transport of goods was economically feasible; (2) the inherently unstable structure and formation of capital; (3) the technical limits to the exploitation of slave labour in large enterprises; (4) the limited degree to which cost accounting was possible, due primarily to the impossibility of strict calculation in the use of slave labour.

It should be noted in passing that private accounting was by no means undeveloped in Antiquity. It was used in banking and also by country estates and extended households to keep inventory. Only the first kind was commercial in character. All other forms of private accounting were – as far as we know – still quite undifferentiated as compared with those of later medieval times, judging by the capitalist standard of how accurately profit margins were reckoned.

Large enterprises based on slave labour were not created in Antiquity for technical reasons – that is, in order to permit production based on division and co-ordination of labour; rather, they arose from purely personal circumstances – the fortuitous accumulation of a large number of slaves in the possession of a single individual. This . . . explains why all large enterprises had a peculiarly unstable, evanescent character. Tax collectors, artisans, shopkeepers – these were the mainstay of the money economy in the Near East and in the Hellenistic states; and when political and economic stability arrived in the West, there too there was a decline in capital formation, and these groups became predominant.

We find repeatedly that it is precisely in the periods of 'hallowed order' – which were also periods of economic stability – that there occurred a swift decline of capitalism. Capitalist entrepreneurs, not to be confused with gentlemen rentiers, generally enjoyed only a rather precarious social position in Antiquity. Conditions differed somewhat at certain periods of Babylonian, Hellenistic, late republican and early imperial Roman history, but certainly in the classical periods proper most entrepreneurs were resident non-citizens and freedmen. Another indication of low status is that men engaged in trade were often ineligible for office, even – or rather, especially – in democracies.

In fact, ancient political theory was based on the ideal of the 'independent citizen', which meant in practice a rentier able to live on his income and also – which was especially important in the 'free' communities – ready to serve in the army whenever needed. Ancient political theory was hostile to the profit motive, but not in the main for reasons similar to those of the medieval church, which condemned impersonal commercial relations because they could not be subjected to ethical norms. Political rather than ethical considerations determined ancient ideas on the subject. Reasons of state, equality of citizens and autarky of the city-state were at the centre of these ideas, and there was also the contempt for trade and tradesmen cultivated by the leisured upper classes.

Businessmen, on the other hand, were not sustained by any positive justification of the profit motive. Only among followers of Cynicism and in the lower middle classes of the Hellenistic Near East do we find the beginnings of such an attitude. In early modern times the rationalisation and economic orientation of life were furthered by the essentially religious idea of 'vocation' and the ethic derived from it, but nothing similar arose in Antiquity. The ancient businessman remained no more than a 'common tradesman' in his own eyes and in the eyes of his contemporaries.

There were of course exceptions, most notably in the area of marine commerce. From the first the ownership of ships and their use to transport goods for sale by employees was 'respectable'; kings, temples and aristocrats in coastal areas engaged in this in early Antiquity. Then there developed genuine mercantile operations involving the use of hired ships to transport purchased or consigned goods to centres of commerce, first as a joint venture and then for the profit of a single organiser. This too was considered respectable, although always with reserve, but only because it involved the irregular use of one's property and did not have the character of an 'established business'; so it does not really weaken our argument.

Another factor which checked the development of capitalism in Antiquity was the great variety of distinctions which divided the population into hereditary classes, especially in the 'free' city-states. Political considerations also caused differentiation in the law of property, especially as it concerned land and inheritance. All of these distinctions could and did become sources of income, equivalent to rents. Especially in the democracies, the interest of the lower-middle classes in safeguarding their incomes and food supply became the dominant factor in city politics; a good example is Athenian citizenship policy. Even in the monarchies this attitude was influential as long as it did not conflict with the state's omnipotent fiscal interests.

3
The Confucianist Bureaucracy and the Germs of Capitalism in China: the City and the Guild

Unlike the cities of the West, those of China and Asia in general had no specific political role. The Asian city was not a *polis* in the Greek or Roman sense. It had no city law such as existed in medieval Europe, for it was not a community with its own political system and privileges. It had no city-dwelling military class possessing its own equipment, such as existed in Western Antiquity. Communities bound by military oath, such as the Compagna Communis and others, which were able to fight against (or negotiate with) the feudal lord of the city to gain autonomy, never existed in Asia. Nor was there an Oriental equivalent of consuls, councils, or political associations of merchant and craft guilds like the Mercanza which owed their existence to the military independence of the city. Revolts by the urban populace which have forced officials to take refuge in the citadel have always been commonplace in the Orient. They have always been aimed, however, at displacing a specific official or decree, especially a new tax, never at gaining a charter, which could guarantee, at least relatively, the freedom of the city.

Clan ties were largely responsible for the inhibition of Eastern city dwellers from seeking autonomy in the Western sense. The immigrant citizen, particularly if he had rural property, retained his relationship with the native place of his clan, its ancestral land and its temple. Thereby all ritually and personally important links with the birthplace were maintained in much the same way as a Russian peasant

59

retained his birthright, with all its concomitant rights and duties, within his own communal village, even if he were a city dweller, permanently occupied as a factory worker, journeyman, merchant, manufacturer, or scholar. The Western city was a community – in Antiquity also a religious association – while during the Middle Ages it was an oath-bound fraternity. China had no equivalent development but only preliminary stages. The Chinese city god was merely a local protective deity, not the god of the community: usually he was a canonised urban mandarin.

Craft and merchant guilds, city leagues and occasionally a 'city guild', similar, on the face of it, to the English Guilda Mercatoria, existed in China until very recent times.

Imperial officials had to take account of the various urban associations, which did, in fact, control to a large extent the economic life of the city. The control which they exercised was, moreover, more thorough than that of the imperial administration, and in many ways than that of the corresponding associations in European cities. In some ways the condition of Chinese cities is reminiscent of their English counterparts in Tudor times, the obvious and important difference being that the English city, at that period, possessed a charter which guaranteed its liberty. In China no such thing existed. In extreme contrast to the West, but analogously to the Indian conditions, the city, as an imperial fortress, enjoyed less formal guarantees of self-government than the village, the latter alone being able to enter freely into political and economic contracts. The city could not file lawsuits and in general could not act as a corporate body. The actual occasional rule of a powerful merchant guild over a city, such as could also be found in India and elsewhere, did not constitute an equivalent of true autonomy.

The explanation of this can be seen when one considers the different origins of the Western and Eastern city. The *polis* of Antiquity began as a city engaged in foreign trade, despite its roots in landlordism. In contrast, China was mainly an inland area.

In spite of the fact that the range of operations of Chinese junks was occasionally quite long and their nautical technology highly developed, overseas trade was of minor importance in comparison with the size of the hinterland. For centuries China had neglected her sea power – a necessary basis of developed trade. Finally, in order to preserve tradition, China confined contact with foreigners to a single port, Canton, and to only thirteen licensed firms. The Imperial Canal, as all the maps and preserved reports show, was built for the sole purpose of avoiding the necessity of transporting rice from south to north by sea with all the risks of piracy and typhoons that that entailed. Even recent official reports state that financial losses incurred by the treasury through sea transport warrant the enormous expenditure involved in reconstructing the canal.

The typical medieval inland Western city, like the Chinese and Middle Eastern city, was usually founded by princes and feudal lords for the purpose of obtaining money, rents and taxes. Yet from early times the European city became a highly privileged association with fixed rights, which were systematically extended because the lord of the city lacked the necessary capacity to administer it, and because the city was a military association which could prevent an army of knights from entering. In contrast the great Middle Eastern cities like Babylon depended for their existence on the royal bureaucracy administering the construction and maintenance of canals from early times. In this respect the Chinese city was much the same, in spite of the looseness of its central administration. The prosperity of the Chinese city was not dependent on the entrepreneurial skills, or political courage and energy, of its citizenry, but rather upon the imperial administration, especially of the waterways. (As the pharaoh's symbol of authority was embodied in his holding the lash in his hand, so the Chinese symbol of governing was the holding of a stick. In the old terminology this was identified with the regulation of waters. The word 'law', *fa*, also means 'the release of water'.)

Western bureaucracy is a recent development and its origins are in part to be found in the autonomous city-states, whereas the Chinese imperial bureaucracy is very ancient. The Chinese city was the planned product of the administration as can be seen from its layout. It had, first of all, its city wall. Secondly, the inhabitants, often insufficient for the fortified area, were brought together, within that wall, often by coercion. As was the case in Egypt, a change of dynasty meant a change of capital, or at least its name. Peking was to become the eventual permanent capital city but until recently its trade and industrial exports were very small.

The looseness of control by the imperial administration meant in fact that both the urban and rural Chinese governed themselves. Occupational associations in the city determined the way of life of their own members, especially those who did not belong to old and powerful clans. Clans also played a decisive role in village life. With the exception of Indian castes, nowhere was the individual so utterly dependent upon craft and merchant guilds as in Chinese cities. With the exception of a few which had an official charter granting a monopoly, the guilds had absolute control over their members without any official licence from the government. Membership of these guilds was obligatory, and those who wished to engage in business activities had to join on pain of death. The guilds owned clubhouses and levied taxes which were a proportion of the official's salary or the merchant's turnover. They punished any member who appealed against another to a court, and provided tombs in a special burial ground intended as a substitute for the native soil. The guilds paid the legal expenses of their members suing outsiders and managed their appeals to central authorities when conflict arose. It goes without saying that they also provided some of the satisfactions of communal life . . .

As well as non-native officials and merchants there were also non-native artisans enrolled in the guilds – there were needle-makers from Kiangsu and Tanchow living in Wenchow. The goldsmiths' guild of Wenchow was made up entirely of natives of Ningpo. The existence of these organisations amounts to a rudimentary ethnic specialisation in crafts. The absolute authority of the guild was an understandable reaction to the always precarious position of guild members in an ethnically foreign environment. It could be likened to the strict, though considerably less rigorous, discipline of the Hansa over the German merchants in London and Novgorod. Local guilds, however, also had almost absolute power over members under pain of expulsion, boycott and lynching. In the nineteenth century a member was bitten to death for disobeying the rule on the maximum number of apprentices he could have! The guild also took charge of such economic matters as weights and measures, currency (made by stamping silver bars), street maintenance, control over the granting of credit and the enforcement of the monopoly. Guilds also supervised deliverers, prosecuted illegal or fictitious transactions, cared for regular repayment of debts, oversaw regulation of rates of exchange, made advances on delayed delivery, regulated the number and conditions of apprentices and guarded secrets of production.

Some guilds controlled funds amounting to millions, which were often invested in joint landholdings. Members were taxed, and entry fees and caution money were demanded from newcomers. The guilds put on theatrical performances, and organised the burial of members fallen on hard times. Charity organisation and joint religious observances were, however, less well developed than in their European counterparts. On the occasions when entry fees were paid to a deity, embodied in the temple treasury, the arrangement offered security against seizure by officials. Poor guilds, unable to pay for a clubhouse of their own, would regularly use a temple as a meeting hall.

Most of the occupational associations were open to all who were employed in their particular trade ... Some, however, were remnants of hereditary monopolies, based on secret crafts of clans and tribes. Certain monopolistic guilds were established by the state for the sake of its fiscal interests or anti-foreign policies. Up to the time of the Nanking Peace thirteen firms monopolised all foreign trade.

The system of compulsory work and deliveries adopted from time to time by the Chinese medieval administration led to the formation of groups of craftsmen compulsorily assigned to their work for the purpose of providing for state needs. Such groups constituted a transitional stage from a specialisation of crafts within clans or tribes (where members were often itinerant) to localised trades with open entry.

In the time of the Han dynasty many industrial activities

were still strictly family secrets. The method of producing Foochow lacquer, for example, died out during the T'ai P'ing rebellion because the clan which alone held the secret of its manufacture was exterminated. As a general rule the cities had no monopoly on manufacturing.

The Emperor and the Mandarins

In China, as in Egypt, the need to control the rivers was a prerequisite for a systematically organised economy. This need was decisive for the rise of a central authority and its patrimonial officialdom, which has been in existence throughout the history of China. Irrigation was already developed when the art of writing emerged and it is possible that the latter evolved out of the administrative needs of the former. Unlike in Egypt and Mesopotamia, however, in northern China (which was the cradle of the empire) priority was given to dyke building against floods, or canal construction for inland water transport, especially of animal feeding stuffs. Canal construction for irrigation was a secondary matter. In Mesopotamia the latter was necessary for the cultivation of desert lands, and river administrators and police formed the basis for the patrimonial bureaucracy.

It may be asked to what extent these circumstances affected not only politics but also religion. The god of the Near East was modelled on the king. The Mesopotamians and Egyptians, who hardly knew rain, believed that the harvest depended upon the activities of the king and his administration: that the king 'created' the harvest. The situation was somewhat similar, though less extreme, in some parts of southern China where the regulation of water was crucial for gardening. However, in northern China natural events, especially rainfall, loomed much larger despite the considerable development of irrigation. In the Middle East the old centralised bureaucratic administration promoted the concept of the supreme deity as a king of the heavens who had 'created' man and the world from nothing, a superhuman ethical ruler who ordained his creatures to do their duty. Only in the Near East has this idea of god imprinted itself with such forcefulness. This fact, however, cannot be deduced solely from economic conditions because the heavenly king also rose to the highest position of power (and finally to an absolute supremacy) in Palestine where, in contrast to the desert regions, rain and sunshine, the sources of fertility, were sent by his grace. Jehovah expressly reminded the Israelites about this. Obviously factors other than the economic played a part in the development of these conceptions of deity . . .

Chinese Antiquity knew a dual god of the peasantry and its local associations who represented a fusion of the spirit of fertile soil and the spirit of harvest. This god had already assumed the character of a deity meting out punishments and rewards. The ancestral spirits were also objects of worship.

The protecting spirit of the local community was in all likelihood first conceived naturalistically as a semi-tangible magical power. It was rather like the local deities of western Asia, but the latter quickly became more personalised. As princely power increased, so the spirit of the ploughland became the spirit of the princely territory. In China, as so often elsewhere, when once a clan of noble heroes developed there appeared a personal god of the heavens resembling the Hellenic Zeus. The founder of the Chou dynasty worshipped such a god of the heavens as well as the local spirit. When the imperial power established its sovereignty over the princes the sacrificial offerings to heaven became the monopoly of the emperor, who came to be seen as the son of heaven. The Chinese spirits, especially the mighty and universal ones, assumed more and more an impersonal character. In the Near East the reverse happened: there the personal almighty creator and royal ruler of the world was promoted above the animist semi-personal spirits and the local deities.

For a long time the concept of God among Chinese philosophers remained contradictory. In the Semitic East, too, the fertile land with natural water was the land of Baal and at the same time his home. He became the god of the local political unit. Fertile land was considered to be the god's property. The Israelite Jehovah was originally a mountain-dwelling god associated with storms and natural catastrophes. He made his presence felt in wartime by appearing as clouds and thunderstorms in order to aid the heroes. He was the unifying god of communities, bound by an oath, whose unity was protected by a contract made with him through the mediation of priests. In this way foreign affairs remained permanently under his jurisdiction and were the concern of his most important prophets, who were also political thinkers at the time when the powerful Mesopotamian robber-states were greatly feared. Jehovah's final image depended on the circumstances. His deeds worked through foreign affairs, determining the outcomes of war and national destinies ... His people, however, unable to create an empire of their own, and finally conquered by the great powers around them, came to conceive their god as a ruler of destiny who stood apart from the world. Even his chosen people had only the significance of creatures who could be blessed or rejected depending on their behaviour. The Chinese World Empire, in contrast, became increasingly pacified despite its distant campaigns and the fact that Chinese culture originated under the influence of pure militarism.

The use of the horse in individual hero combat in China and elsewhere led to the disintegration of the men's house of foot soldiers. The horse was first used to pull war chariots and this was instrumental in the rise of combat between individual heroes, well versed in military arts and equipped with expensive arms. This 'Homeric' age of China was very remote in time. In China, Egypt and Mesopotamia knightly combat did not lead to an individualist social order as strong as that of the Homeric Hellas or the Western Middle Ages. Presumably the main reason why this did not happen was the Chinese dependence on river regulation and consequent bureaucratic management by the prince. As in India, each district was obliged to provide war chariots and armed men. There was, therefore, no personal contact like that of the Western medieval vassalage. The increasing importance of steady work militated against the development of the notion of a heaven populated by warrior deities. The Chinese emperor executed the rite of ploughing; having become the patron saint of ploughing, he was no more a warrior prince

BUREAUCRACY AND THE GERMS OF CAPITALISM IN CHINA

... From the time when the scholars began to rule the ideology tended to become increasingly pacifist.

In contrast to the Holy Roman Empire in medieval Europe, the imperial lord paramount was also a high priest during the feudal era in China. As a high priest the emperor was an essential element of cultural cohesion among the individual states which varied in size, power and homogeneity. A ritual confirmed this cohesion. In China, as in the Western Middle Ages, religious unity permitted the interstate mobility of noble families. The noble stateman was free to transfer his services from one prince to another.

The unification of the Chinese Empire, which took place in the third century BC and which was reversed only intermittently afterwards, produced at the same time the internal pacification of the empire. Defence against and the subjection of the barbarians became merely a governmental police duty. The god of heaven in China, consequently, did not assume (as in Israel) the form of a hero-god who revealed his powers by determining the destiny of his people in war, victory, defeat and exile. Usurpation of the throne or invasion merely led to the appointment of a different tax collector, not to a different social order ... A strictly bureaucratic order developed, with open recruitment to office ... It was not accidental that history ascribes the earliest sale of office to the first emperor, Shih Huang Ti. This practice necessarily brought wealthy plebeians into offices of the state. Opportunities for officials of low birth increased when a hierarchy of offices was established, the beginnings of which began in the warring states. Until the feudal powers had been overcome by the new imperial authority with the aid of plebeian forces, men of plebeian origins could only become politically influential within the scholarly class, and then only under special conditions.

Since the beginning of the administrative rationalisation, the Annals of the warring states give examples of princes' plenipotentiaries who were of poor and common descent and who owed their position entirely to their knowledge. The scholars, because of their ability and mastery of ritual, claimed preference for supreme offices, even above the princes' next-of-kin – a claim contested by the vassals. The scholars, therefore, found themselves in unofficial positions, like ministers without portfolio, resembling father-confessors to the prince.

As in the West, the feudal nobility opposed the admission of strangers to posts which they tried to monopolise – hence the struggle between the scholars and the nobility. During the early part of Shih Huang Ti's rule, and before the unification of the empire, it is recorded that in the year 237 BC foreign-born scholars and traders were expelled. However, the ruler's interest in power led him to revoke this measure and from then on his first minister was a man of letters, who described himself as a self-made man of lowly origins. Following the unification of the empire . . . and with the growth of anti-traditionalist and systematic absolutism, the autocrat turned against the power of the . . . mandarin scholars . . .

The emperor attempted to destroy all classical literature and the institution of scholarship itself by burning the sacred books and allegedly burning alive 460 scholars, thus introducing pure absolutism – a rule based on personal favourites with no consideration for descent or education. It culminated in the nomination of a eunuch as the grand master of the household and tutor to the second son. The favouritism of purely Oriental sultanism which combined status-levelling and absolute autocracy appeared to become the order of the day in China. It was a system against which the aristocracy of cultured scholars were to fight, with varying degrees of success, for centuries . . .

The tremendous increase in forced labour for imperial building works demanded, as in the empire of the pharaohs, a relentless and unlimited control of the labour force and the tax revenue of the land. However, the all-powerful palace eunuch of Shih Huang Ti's successor is said to have recommended that the ruler ally himself with 'the people' and appoint officials without regard for either social position or education, saying: 'It is now the time for the rule of the sword, not fine manner.' This advice accords perfectly with typical Oriental patrimonialism. The emperor, however, did not follow the magician's advice to make himself 'invisible' for the sake of raising his prestige. This would have meant his internment like the Dalai Lama's and would have placed his administration entirely in the grip of officials. He maintained 'autocratic rule' in the true sense: that is, by himself.

A violent reaction against this harsh sultanism came from the old families, intellectuals, the army angry over building duties and the peasant class, overburdened by taxation, military service and unpaid labour. The leaders were men of humble origins: Chen Shi, the leader of the army revolt, was a peasant. The leader of the peasants and founder of the Han dynasty, Lu Pang, was a field watchman in a village. His power grew from an alliance of his clan with other peasant clans. Thus it was not a man from the genteel strata of society, but an upstart, who brought about the fall of a dynasty and founded a new one which reunited the realm after its disintegration. The final victory, however, fell to the scholars, whose rational administrative and economic policies were again decisive in restoring imperial authority. They were also more efficient administrators than the favourites and eunuchs whom they constantly opposed. Above all they enjoyed and exploited the tremendous prestige associated with the knowledge of precedent, ritual and scripture which was at that time something of a secret art.

Figures of published registrations reveal that officials usually understated the taxable area of land and the number of actual taxpayers by about 40 per cent unless the ruler was exceptionally vigilant and energetic. Local and provincial costs naturally had to be deducted so that a very fluctuating revenue remained for the central authorities. From the eighteenth century until recent times, the governors (like the Persian satraps) transferred tribute, usually fixed in lump sums. The levying of taxes by fixed lump sums had wide implications for the power of the provincial governors, who nominated, or put forward for appointment to central authorities, most of the district officials . . . The empire resembled a confederation of provincial governorships under a pontifical head.

The emperors cleverly employed typical patrimonialist methods for maintaining their personal power. Among these were short assignments lasting three years, after which the official was transferred to a different province. Officials could not hold office in their home province, nor could their relatives be employed in the same district. The so-called censors constituted a systematic network of surveillance. Nevertheless, all such measures failed to establish a thoroughly unified administration . . . The central authorities had no clear insight into provincial finances . . . Until recently provincial governors could conclude treaties with foreign powers since the central government was not sufficiently organised to do so. Furthermore, practically all important administrative orders which appeared to be sent by provincial governors were in fact issued by their unofficial subordinates. Until recently subordinate authorities often regarded the decrees of the central government as expressions of moral advice or desire rather than as orders; and although an individual official could be removed at any time this did not really benefit the central authorities. The fact that an official was prohibited from holding office in his home province and had to shift to a new post every three years was enough to prevent his becoming independently powerful in the manner of the feudal vassals. These measures contributed to the external unity of the empire at the cost of the official never really being fully rooted in his district.

The mandarin, accompanied by a whole flock of his clansmen, friends and personal clients, took up office in a strange province. He was frequently from the beginning dependent on an interpreter's services, being unable to understand the dialect. In addition, because of his lack of knowledge of the provincial law, which was based on precedent, he could incur danger by violating its sacred traditions. He was therefore entirely dependent on the instructions of an unofficial adviser who was a native, a man of letters and well versed in local customs, and who played the role of a 'father confessor' whom the official treated with respect, often devotion, calling him his 'teacher'. In addition to this the official was dependent on unofficial assistants whom he was obliged to pay from his own pocket. Whereas the official staff in the pay of the state had to be born outside the province, these unofficial assistants were recruited from among qualified natives of the province. It was necessary to rely on such men, not yet appointed to office, as they had knowledge of the local situation which the new official lacked . . . The consequences of all this were inevitably that real power lay in the hands of unofficial, native subordinates. The higher the rank of the official, the more he lacked sufficient information about the local conditions needed for consistent and rational intervention.

The emancipation of officials from control by the central authority, and the emergence of feudalism, were prevented under Chinese patrimonialism by a famous and extremely efficient method: namely, the introduction of examinations and selection for office on the basis of educational merit rather than birth or rank. This was of decisive importance for Chinese administration and culture . . . but the mentality of the bureaucracy differed greatly between the East and the West.

The form which Chinese bureaucracy took was connected with the system of public taxation, as this developed, depending on the fluctuations of the monetary economy . . . It would seem that, according to their original names, taxes developed partly from customary gifts, partly from the obligatory tributes of subject peoples and partly from the leasing of Crown lands. Public land, obligatory tax and forced labour coexisted all the time and were variously interrelated. Whichever gained ascendancy depended, in part, on the state of the (very unstable) currency, on the degree of pacification and on the reliability of the bureaucratic machine.

According to a legend, the 'holy' Emperor Yü instituted the regulation of rivers and the construction of canals, while Shih Huang Ti, the first emperor to rule through a genuine bureaucracy, was reckoned to be the greatest builder of canals, roads, fortifications and, above all, of the Great Wall, though in fact he brought it only to partial completion. Such legend vividly expresses the origins of the patrimonial bureaucracy in flood control and the construction of canals. The ruler's power is derived from the compulsory labour of his subjects, which was as essential for the control of floods in China as it was in Egypt and the Near East.

Any interference in the traditional economy and administration affected the wide network of the interests of the ruling classes in their rights to collect fees and levies. Since officials could be demoted to a less remunerative post, officialdom banded together to resist, as strongly as the taxpayer, all attempts to change the system of fees, tariffs, or tax payments. Only a violent revolution from above or below could have changed this. One can realise on looking at the reforms intended by the emperor in 1898 that even their partial execution would have produced tremendous changes in the relative incomes of the officials. One can judge, then, the complete hopelessness of this attempt, because too many vested interests opposed it and because no independent, disinterested bodies existed outside those groups.

It is, in principle, important to realise that, contrary to what one might expect, the purely patrimonial political formations, to which category most Oriental states belonged, did not follow the same pattern of development. Thus the money economy, rather than weakening traditionalism, did in fact strengthen it, because the money economy, connected with taxation, created special opportunities for the ruling classes to make profits. Generally speaking it strengthened their rentier mentality and their interest in maintaining the economic conditions, which permitted them to collect fees and levies. With each step towards a money economy in Egypt, the Islamic states and China we see an increase in the practice of the leasing of rights to local officials to levy taxes. After short transitional periods when the appropriation of these rights was not yet completed, this process produced ossification. A general result of Oriental patrimonialism, with its tax-leasing practices, was that as a rule only military conquest from outside or military or religious revolutions could break the firm structure of tax-leasing interests, and create new power structures and new economic conditions. All attempts at internal innovation were doomed by the aforementioned obstacles. Modern Europe is a great historical exception to this largely because it was never pacified under one empire. We must remember that the same class of tax collectors which prevented the streamlining of administration in the unified Chinese Empire was promoting it in the warring smaller kingdoms.

Just as competition for markets compelled the rationalisation of private enterprise, interstate rivalry necessitated the rationalisation of the state economy and economic policy in the West as in China at the time of the warring kingdoms. In a market economy, cartelisation weakens rational calculation, which is the essence of capitalism: likewise, the disappearance of rivalry among states weakened the stimulus to rational management of administration, finance and economic policy. Even at the time of interstate rivalry in China the rationalisation of administration and the economy was much more limited than in the West, where princely power allied itself with other forces to break the bonds of tradition. In certain circumstances these forces could use their own military strength to overcome the patrimonial power. This happened in the five great revolutions which decided the destiny of the West: the Italian Revolution of the twelfth and thirteenth centuries, the Netherlands' Revolution of the sixteenth century, the English Revolution of the seventeenth century and the French and American Revolutions of the eighteenth century. We can ask ourselves, 'Were there no comparable forces in China? . . .'.

The intense acquisitiveness of the Chinese people has, without doubt, been highly developed for a long time. Ruthless competitiveness towards those outside their own clan was extremely common among them . . . The incomparable Chinese capacity for industry and hard work has always been well recognised. The merchant guilds, as we have already remarked, were more powerful than in many other countries and their autonomy was almost unlimited. The tremendous growth of the Chinese population since the early eighteenth century and the steadily growing abundance of precious metals would seem, by European standards, to have provided favourable conditions for the development of capitalism. But here we must return to our original problem: although we have found some reasons for the fact that capitalism did not develop, we have no satisfactory answers as yet.

For twelve centuries social position was determined by qualification for office rather than by wealth. This qualification was, in turn, determined by education, particularly by examination results. China made literary scholarship the criterion for social prestige far more than Germany, or Europe in the period of the humanists . . . Scholars in China were the decisive exponents of unity in culture, like the Brahmans in India. Territories (and enclaves) not administered by scholarly officials, educated according to the orthodox state model, were seen as heterodox and barbarian. This was not unlike the Brahmans' attitude to Hindu lands not governed by themselves or that of the Greeks towards a territory not organised as a *polis* . . . The social character of the educated classes determined their attitude towards economic policy . . . a permanent aversion to the purely economic differentiation of status brought about through transactions on a free market. Such aversions are common to all bureaucracies. The world empire's increasingly stable economic situation, with its self-sufficiency and homogeneous social structure, did not give rise to the sort of economic problems that were discussed in seventeenth-century English literature. There was no rising bourgeoisie, conscious of its power and position, which the government could not ignore. There were no expansive capitalist interests of sufficient strength, as was the case in England, which could be capable of forcing the government into their service.

The whole picture of the scholars' situation can be understood only when one considers the forces against which they had to fight. In early times their main enemies were the 'great families' of the feudal period, who did not want to lose the monopoly of their offices. Later there were the capitalists who bought office, as a natural result of the levelling of privileges and of the fiscal need for money.

Scholars also had to resist the ruler's interest in efficiency, which might have lead to their replacement by expert officialdom. Specialist, expert officials came to the fore as early as 601 during the reign of Wen Ti. During the stress of the defensive wars in 1068 under Wang An-Shih, they enjoyed total success albeit short-lived. However, tradition finally triumphed and this time for good.

There still remained one major and permanent enemy of the scholars. This was sultanism and the eunuch system which supported it. The Confucians, therefore, viewed the influence of the harem with deep suspicion. Without some knowledge of this struggle, Chinese history is extremely difficult to understand. The never-ending struggle of the scholars against sultanism lasted for two millennia and began in the time of Shih Huang Ti. It was carried on under the dynasties. It was understandable that energetic rulers continually sought to gain independence from the cultured scholars through reliance on eunuchs and plebeian climbers. Many scholars who made a stand against absolutism sacrificed their lives to maintain their class in power. In the long run, however, the literati triumphed over and over again, for drought, flood, eclipses of the sun, or military defeat and in fact every generally threatening event immediately placed power in their hands. Such events were seen as a consequence of a breach of tradition and a deviation from the classic way of life, which the scholars guarded. In all such circumstances 'free discussion' was permitted, the advice of the king was sought and the inevitable result was the cessation of the non-classical form of government, execution or exile of the eunuchs, a return to the classical ways and concessions to the demands of the scholars . . .

During the period of the warring kingdoms and their struggle for political power there existed a capitalism of money-lenders and traders which was politically oriented and seemingly very significant. High profit margins seem to have been the norm. In China, as in other patrimonial states, this form of capitalism was common. As well as transactions concerning politics, mining and trade are also mentioned as ways by which wealth could be accumulated. Multimillionaires (on a copper standard) are said to have existed during the time of the Han dynasty. However, when China was unified into a world empire like Imperial Rome, this capitalism suffered obvious regression, for it was essentially linked with competition between states. Conversely, the development of pure market capitalism, seeking opportunity for free trading, was only rudimentary. In industry itself the merchant's status was obviously superior to that of the technician. This was also the case with co-operative forms of enterprise . . . The predominance of the merchant is clearly demonstrated in the way profit was normally distributed within associations. Interlocal industries often yielded considerable speculative gains. The old classical esteem for the sacred vocation of agriculture, even during the first century BC, did not prevent profit opportunities being deemed greater in industry and greatest in trade. Passages in the Talmud suggest that a similar development occurred in the Near East.

This type of capitalist activity, however, did not give rise to modern capitalism. To this day those institutions which the prosperous burghers of medieval Europe developed are absent in China. The legal and societal foundations for capitalist 'enterprise' were missing in the Chinese economy. As usually happened in patrimonial states, the officials with the right to collect taxes had the best opportunities to accumulate wealth . . .

Retired officials used their fortunes more or less legally acquired for the purchase of landholdings. Their sons, to preserve their wealth and influence, remained in hereditary partnership as joint heirs and in turn raised the means for some members of the family to study. These students gained the opportunity of entering remunerative offices and they, in turn, were expected to enrich their relatives and provide public employment for their clan members. Property was acquired through politics and there developed a group of land magnates who leased estates. This unstable patriciate was neither feudal nor bourgeois, but speculated in opportunities for the purely political exploitation of office . . . It is obvious that this type of acquisitive familial community was a development quite unlike the rational, economic, corporate enterprise. Above all, this community was united by rigid kinship bonds, which leads us on to discuss the significance of the clan.

The Clan

The clan, which in medieval Europe was practically extinct, was preserved fully in China. In the administration of the districts it functioned together with the economic associations, developing to an extent unknown elsewhere, even in India. The patrimonial rule from above encountered the clans' powerful influence from below. Up to the present time, many of the dangerous political 'secret societies' have been clans. Villages were often named after the clan which exclusively or predominantly resided there. Sometimes village societies were confederations or clans. Old boundary marks suggest that land was allotted not to individuals but to clans. The cohesiveness of the clan was important for maintaining this state of affairs.

The village headman (who was often paid) was elected from the clan which was most powerful numerically. The elders of the clan had the right to depose him . . . Clan cohesion was undoubtedly based on the cult of ancestors. The clan resisted the ruthless encroachments of the patrimonial administration, its impositions, its resettlements and redistributions of land and the registration of individuals in groups of joint liability for service. Ancestor worship was the sole folk cult that was not controlled by the Caesaropapist government* and its officials. The head of the household, who was also a homepriest, was assisted by the family in his duties . . . It was believed to be absolutely necessary to satisfy the spirits and win their favour by offering sacrifices . . . Ancestral spirits of emperors were of almost equal rank with the heavenly spirit. A Chinese without a male heir was obliged to resort to adoption, and if he had failed to do so then the family undertook a posthumous and fictitious adoption on his behalf. This was not so much for his sake as for their own since they wanted to be at peace with his spirit. The social consequences of these extremely widely held ideas are evident in the tremendous support gained by patriarchal power, and in the

* A government whose head is also the chief of the religious hierarchy. (S.A.)

strengthening of clan cohesion. In Egypt it was the cult of the dead rather than the ancestral cult which dominated everything. There, clan cohesion was shattered under the influence of bureaucratisation and fiscalism, as it was later broken in Mesopotamia. In China, however, the influence of the clan was maintained and grew to balance the prerogatives of the overlord.

Every clan has its ancestral hall which often contains a tablet with the customary laws recognised by the clan which has the unquestionable right to impose them upon its members. Although joint liability was confined to criminal law, the clan settled the debts of its members whenever possible. Only the clan was clearly obliged to aid the needy and to give loans. If the need arose the clan waged feuds against outsiders. Here, where personal interest and personal ties were involved, the relentless bravery of the Chinese contrasted most glaringly with the much vaunted 'cowardice' of the government's army which consisted of impressed recruits or mercenaries. Where necessary, again, the clan provided medicaments, doctors and burial services; it cared for the aged and widows and, above all, it provided schools.

The clan owned property, especially landed property, and prosperous clans often held extensive lands in trust. The clan utilised this land by leasing it out (usually for three years, by auction), but sale of such land was permissible only with the consent of three-quarters of the clan. The yield was distributed among the heads of the households. The typical method of this distribution was to give all men and all widows one unit each; then from the age of 59 on, two units; from 69 on, three units.

All married men had an equal vote, while unmarried men had only the right to be heard in council, and women were excluded from the clan's councils, as well as from the right of inheritance. The governing council consisted of the elders, each representing a separate lineage within the clan. The elders were, however, annually elected by a vote of all clan members. The functions of the elders were to collect revenues, to organise the use of the common possessions, distribute income and, most important of all, attend to the ancestral sacrifices, the ancestral halls and schools.

... Below the level of the *hsien* district, which was about the size of an English county, there were only those governing agents who were, officially, honorific officeholders, and in fact often prosperous peasants. But very frequently committees functioned alongside the official administration of the districts right up to the level of the province. Officially the committees were appointed or given 'delegated' authority for a three-year term and were subject to recall at any time. Actually, they held their positions through recognised or *de facto* acquired influence, and they 'gave advice' to the officials.

It was necessary to reach agreement with this body, a firmly cohesive stratum of village notables, whenever any change whatsoever was to be introduced, such as, for instance, raising the traditional taxes. Otherwise the state official was just as certain of meeting stubborn resistance as were the landlord, lessor, employer and in general any 'superior' outside the clan. The clan stood as one man in support of any member who felt wronged and the joint resistance of the clan was naturally much more effective than a strike by a freely formed trade union in the Occident. By this alone, 'work discipline' and the selection of labour on a free market, characteristic of modern large enterprise, have been thwarted in China.

... A considerable measure of usurped or conceded self-government faced the patrimonial bureaucracy. On the one hand there were the clans and on the other the organisations of the village poor. The rationalism of the bureaucracy was confronted with a resolute and traditionalistic power which, on the whole and in the long run, was stronger because it operated continuously and rested upon the most intimate personal associations. Moreover, any innovation could call forth magic evil powers ... This tremendous power of the strictly patriarchical clan was, in truth, the carrier of the much-discussed 'democracy' of China, which had nothing whatsoever in common with 'modern' democracy. It was rather the outcome, first of the abolition of feudal hereditary ranks, secondly, of the extended character of the patrimonial bureaucratic administration, and thirdly, of the unbroken vigour and power of the patriarchical clans.

The Impact of the Social Structure on the Economy

Economic organisations which went beyond the scope of the individual establishment rested almost wholly upon actual or fictitious clan relationships . . . In the cities, besides the shops of individual artisans, there were specialised business associations. Small-capitalist in nature, these were organised as communal workshops with a thorough division of manual labour. Technical and commercial management was often specialised and profits were distributed partly according to the contributions to capital and partly according to the value of commercial or technical services. Similar arrangements have been known in Hellenistic Antiquity and the Islamic Middle Ages. In China such establishments were founded probably to make it easier to endure slack periods in seasonal industries and, of course, to facilitate credit and the specialisation of productive work.

The social aspects of large economic units had a specifically democratic character. They protected the individual against the danger of proletarianisation and subjection by capitalists. Such domination, however, could creep in through high investments by absentee capitalists and through the superior power and higher shares in profit enjoyed by sales managers. However, the putting-out system, which introduced capitalist domination in the West, has in China apparently been confined until the present time to the various forms of irregular dependence of the artisan on the merchant. Only in certain trades did it reach the stage of domestic work with dispersed shops for finishing work and a central sales depot. At present the putting-out system has developed on a significant scale only in trades working for distant markets. The decisive circumstance may have been that there was very little opportunity of coercing the dependent workers and getting them to deliver on time goods of the prescribed quantity and quality. Probably no factories producing mass consumers' goods have ever existed since there was no steady market for them. Except in the case of silk, the manufacturers could hardly compete with the domestic industry even on distant markets. Long-distance trade in silk, however, was monopolised by the caravans of the imperial household. Because of the low productivity of the mines the metal industry could develop only on a modest scale. There are pictorial representations of large plants with specialisation of labour for the processing of tea. They resemble ancient Egyptian pictures. The manufacturing establishments owned by the state usually produced luxury goods, as in Islamic Egypt . . .

The guilds regulated apprenticeship, but there are no traces of journeymen's associations. Only in individual cases did the workers combine against the masters and go on strike; otherwise they had scarcely begun to develop into a separate class, which (for similar reasons) was also the case in Russia thirty years ago.* As far as is known the workers were members of the guilds with equal rights. The absence of monopolistic exclusion of apprentices in the guild was in harmony with the handicraft nature of the trade which was not even petty capitalist. Hereditary closure and state bondage of occupations emerged repeatedly and were apparently maintained for a time. This might have led to formation of castes, but did not. The Annals mention an attempt of this kind which was made towards the end of the sixth century and ended in failure. Remnants of magically 'unclean' tribes and occupations did survive. Commonly, nine kinds of degraded 'castes' were distinguished: certain kinds of slaves, descendants of such slaves and serfs, beggars, descendants of former rebels, descendants of immigrant barbarians (guest tribes), musicians and performers who played at family ceremonies, actors and jugglers as in medieval Europe . . . Slavery came in after the wars of conquest, through surrender or sale by parents, or as a form of punishment by the government. As in the Occident, the freed man had to obey his patron and was unable to acquire degrees through examinations. During their period of service contract labourers had to be obedient to their masters and were not allowed to eat with them . . .

There was no hereditary stratification among the Chinese

* That is, around 1880. (S.A.)

during the modern period, apart from a titular nobility. This leaves aside the strict segregation of the families registered in the Manchu army, an aspect of the foreign rule which came into existence in the seventeenth century. As early as the eighteenth century the 'bourgeois' mercantile class had succeeded in loosening the fetters of the police state. In the nineteenth century there was free residential mobility which could be traced a long way back. Freedom to settle and purchase land outside one's native community had been promulgated by the fiscal authorities, as in the Occident. From 1794 membership in a new community could be obtained by acquiring real estate and paying taxes for twenty years which entailed forfeiting membership in one's native community. Despite the Sacred Edict of 1671 which recommended adherence to one's occupation, choice of occupations has been free for a long time. In the modern period we find no compulsory passports, schooling, or military service. There are no laws restraining usury nor any similar legal restrictions on trade. Although this state of affairs seems to have been very favourable to a free development of profitable business enterprise it produced no bourgeoisie of the Occidental type. Even those forms of capitalist enterprise which were similar to those known in the Occident during the Middle Ages failed to mature. From a purely economic point of view it might appear that a genuine bourgeois, industrial capitalism could have developed from the petty capitalist beginnings we have discussed above. A number of reasons have already been given why capitalism failed to develop. Nearly all of them stemmed from the structure of the state.

The patrimonial nature of administration and legislation created a realm of unshakeable sacred tradition alongside a realm of arbitrariness and favouritism. These political factors impeded development of industrial capitalism, sensitive to the lack of rational and calculable administration and law enforcement, whether in China, India, Islam, or elsewhere. The development of rational enactment and adjudication of law in the West was facilitated by the principle that the royal prerogative can over-ride common law. However, this principle could not benefit the development of capitalist legal institutions in China (as it had done in the Occidental Middle Ages), because the cities lacked corporate political autonomy, and indispensable legal institutions, fixed and guaranteed by a charter, did not exist. The latter factors, in combination, and with the aid of the aforementioned principle, have created all the legal arrangements appropriate to capitalism in the medieval Occident . . . The German emperors of the Middle Ages enacted a mass of statutes in which the legal provisions were notable for their relatively brief and businesslike form.

These laws stood in contrast to the patriarchal commandments and admonitions of the Buddhist monarchs of India where ethical and administrative decrees resembled some of the Chinese statutes. The Chinese statutes were also systematically collected in the Book of Laws, *Ta Ch'ing Lu Li*, but they contained few and only indirectly pertinent laws covering subjects of greatest importance for commerce. No fundamental freedoms of the individual were guaranteed. In one case among the warring states (the state of Ch'en, 563 BC) the rationalism of the scholarly officials prompted a codification of the laws engraved on metal plates. But according to the Annals, when the question was discussed among the scholars a minister of the state of Ch'in successfully objected: 'If the people can read, they will despise their superiors.'. . .

Though formally under separate secretaries for taxation and for justice, administration and legal proceedings were not in practice separated. In patrimonial fashion the mandarin hired domestic servants at his own expense for both police work and minor office duties. The basically antiformalist and patriarchal character of mandarin administration is unmistakable – offensive behaviour was punished even in the absence of specific prohibitions. Most significant was the moralistic character of patrimonial adjudication which, being ethically oriented, sought justice rather than formal conformity with the law . . .

Capital investment in industry is far too sensitive to such irrational use of authority and too dependent upon the possibility of calculating in advance the steady and rational operation of the state machinery to emerge under a government of this type. But the decisive question is, why did this administration and judiciary remain so irrational from a capitalist point of view? . . .

The states of the Occident had to compete for freely mobile capital in Antiquity (until the establishment of the world empire) as well as during the Middle Ages and modern times. As in the Roman Empire, political competition for capital disappeared following the unification of the Chinese Empire. The Chinese Empire also lacked overseas and colonial relations and this handicapped the development of those types of capitalism common to Occidental Antiquity, the Middle Ages and modern times. These were the varieties of booty capitalism, represented by colonial capitalism and by Mediterranean overseas capitalism connected with piracy. While the barriers to overseas expansion partly depended on the geographical conditions of a great inland empire, in part, as we have seen, they resulted from the general political and economic character of Chinese society.

Rational industrial capitalism, which in the Occident found its specific locus in manufacturing, has been handicapped not only by the lack of a formally guaranteed law, a rational administration and judiciary, and by the ramifications of a system of rights to collect revenue, but also, basically, by the lack of spiritual foundations. Above all it has been handicapped by the attitude rooted in the Chinese 'ethos' and peculiar to a class of officials and aspirants to office.

4
Hindu Religion, Caste and Bureaucratic Despotism as Factors of Economic Stagnation: the Caste and the Tribe

In contrast to China, India has been, and remains, a land of villages and of immutable hereditary organisation. At the same time, however, it was a land of commerce: foreign, particularly with the Occident, as well as internal. Trade, credit and usury have existed in India since ancient Babylonian times. In the north-west Indian commerce received considerable Hellenic influence. At an early period the Jews settled in the south. Zarathustrians from Persia settled in the north-west, constituting a group wholly devoted to wholesale trade. Into this situation came the influence of Islam and the rationalistic enlightenment of the Great Mogul Akbar. Under the Great Moguls, and also during several periods before them, all or almost all of India formed one political unit. Such periods of unity were interrupted, however, by long periods of distintegration when the country was divided into numerous, constantly warring, states.

The methods of warfare, politics and finance of the princes were rationalised and became the subject of theorising – in the case of politics, of a quite Machiavellian kind. Knightly combat as well as the disciplined army equipped by the prince appeared. Although the use of artillery did not develop here earlier than elsewhere, as is occasionally maintained, it appeared early. State creditors, tax farming, state contracting, trade and transport monopolies, and so on, developed along lines parallel to the Occidental patrimonial pattern. For centuries urban development in India resembled that of the Occident on many points. Our contemporary rational number system, the technical basis of all 'calculability', is of Indian origin. The zero was invented sometime in the fifth or sixth century AD. Arithmetic and algebra are considered to have been independently developed in India. For negative magnitudes the term 'ksaya' (debts) was used. In contrast to the Chinese, the Indians cultivated rational science (including mathematics and grammar). They developed numerous philosophic schools and religious sects of almost all possible sociological types . . . For long periods tolerance towards religious and philosophic doctrines was almost absolute; at least it was infinitely greater than anywhere in the Occident until very recent times.

Indian justice developed numerous procedures which could have served capitalistic purposes as easily and well as corresponding institutions of our own medieval law. The legislative autonomy of the merchant class was at least as wide as that of our medieval merchants. Indian handicrafts and occupational specialisation were highly developed. The acquisitiveness of Indians of all strata left little to be improved upon and nowhere is there to be found so little condemnation of and such high regard for wealth. Yet no indigenous modern capitalism developed either before or during English rule. It was taken over as a finished artefact without independent beginnings. We shall inquire here how Indian religion may have prevented capitalistic development as one factor among many . . .

Usually the spread of Hinduism occurs in more or less the following way. The leading group of an 'animistic' tribal territory begins to imitate specific Hindu customs in roughly the following order: abstention from meat, particularly beef; absolute refusal to slaughter cows; total abstinence from intoxicating drinks. Certain other specific practices of purification of good Hindu castes may be added. The ruling stratum gives up marriage practices which diverge from Hindu custom and organises itself into exogamous sibs, forbidding the marriage of its daughters to men of inferior ranks . . . The adoption of additional Hindu customs follows rapidly: restrictions are placed upon contacts and commensality; widows are forced into celibacy; daughters are given in marriage before puberty without their consent; the dead are cremated rather than buried; sacrifices for dead ancestors come into practice; and native deities are re-baptised with the names of Hindu gods and goddesses. Finally, tribal priests are eliminated and a Brahman is requested to take charge of the rituals . . .

'Guest peoples' lived in all parts of the Hindu community. They can still be found today. Still present among us are the gypsies, a typical ancient Indian guest people who, in contrast to others, have wandered beyond India. In earlier times similar phenomena were much more common in India. As elsewhere a guest people does not primarily appear as absolutely homeless. More commonly the guest peoples come from tribes which still possess villages of their own, but sell the products of their household or tribal industry interlocally; or from tribes whose members periodically hire themselves outside as harvesters, day labourers, repair men, servants, or, finally, from tribes which traditionally monopolise interlocal trade in some product.

The natural increase of the . . . barbarian tribes, coupled with the increasing demand for labour in the developing centres of culture with their increasing wealth, gave rise to numerous lower or unclean occupations. As the local resident population shunned them, these occupations fell into the hands of alien workers of foreign origin who inhabited urban areas but retained their tribal affiliations.

. . . Commonly, the guest workers are excluded from intermarriage and commensalism, and are held to be ritually 'impure'. When there are such ritual barriers against a guest people, we shall call them 'pariah people' . . .

The term 'pariah people' in this special sense should not be applied to any tribe treated by a local community as 'strange', 'barbaric', or 'magically impure' unless they are at the same time wholly or predominantly a guest people.

The purest form of this type is found when the people in question have totally lost their residential anchorage and hence are completely occupied performing services for other peoples – the gypsies, for instance, or, in another way, the Jews of the Middle Ages.

The transition from guest workers to a pariah people is accomplished by numerous stages. In every village may be found certain guest workers such as those who prepare cow hides and leather – who, despite their indispensability have, for a millennium, been treated as absolutely impure. By their very presence they infect the air of a room, and so defile food in it that it must be thrown away. A ritualistic contamination by a man of impure caste may even destroy the sexual potency of a Brahman . . . While impure guest workers have been excluded since ancient times from the village community, they are not thereby made into outlaws. The village gives them a definite reward for their services and reserves for them a monopoly in their occupations . . .

There are various degrees of Hinduisation, that is, the transformation of tribes into castes; sometimes subdivisions of a tribe are settled as a guest people among several castes, while the remaining subdivisions continue to exist without losing their tribal organisation.

Usually Hinduisation advances in the form of a slow absorption of whole groups, as individuals can never affiliate directly with that community except as a group; and since affiliation always rests on the fiction that the respective group has always been a caste, it offers a parallel to the way in which a Catholic dogma is never newly enacted like a modern law, but 'found' and 'defined' as having always been valid. Thus the hereditary principle of Hindu religion is upheld.

What were, and are, the motives prompting assimilation? The Brahmans, acting as intermediaries, have an interest in expanding their income, ranging from fees for horoscopes to gifts of cattle, money, jewellery and, above all, land and land rent as compensations for providing 'proofs' of respectable descent for the ruling stratum in an area undergoing assimilation.

What could be the motives of the group desiring assimilation? The tribes which were transformed into 'castes', particularly their ruling ranks, had to accept a yoke of rituals unmatched elsewhere in the world. They had to give up pleasures – for instance, alcohol – which are usually relinquished only with great reluctance. What, then, was the reason?

Legitimation by religion has always been decisive for an alliance between politically and socially dominant classes and the priesthood. Integration into the Hindu community not only endowed the ruling stratum of the barbarians with a respectable rank in the world of Hinduism, but, through their transformation into castes, secured their superiority over the subject classes with an efficiency unsurpassed by any other religion.

In ancient times it was the kings who took the lead in bringing about Hinduisation. As the Slavic kings of Eastern Europe invited into their lands German priests, knights, merchants and peasants, so the kings of the East Ganges Plain and of southern India called in Brahmans skilled in writing and administration. Their services were enlisted to assist the prince in organising his patrimonial bureaucratic administration and ranking according to the formal Hindu pattern and to consecrate the position of the prince as a raja or maharaja.

. . . Hinduism was a well-nigh irresistible social force. Only two salvation religions clearly hostile to the Brahmans – Jainism and, to a greater extent, Buddhism – have opposed Hinduism within the area of the Indian culture . . . Eventually they were completely defeated.

Truly sanguine persecutions of these heterodoxies were not absent during the Hindu restoration, but they obviously do not account for the unusually easy victory of Hinduism. Political circumstances contributed to this victory, but a crucial factor was Hinduism's ability to provide an incomparable religious legitimation of the status of the ruling strata in the social conditions of India. The religions of salvation were unable to supply such support.

. . . Once Hinduism is established, its assimilative power is so great that it can integrate social forms from beyond its religious boundaries. Thus, deliberately anti-Brahmanical and anti-caste religious movements, contradicting some of the fundamentals of Hinduism, have ended as parts of the caste order.

The process is not hard to explain. When a sect which rejects the caste system, recruits members from various Hindu castes and tears them away from their ritualistic duties, the orthodox respond by excommunicating all the sect's proselytes. Unable to abolish the system, the sect becomes a quasi-guest folk, another caste in the Hindu order . . .

Although caste is absolutely essential for every Hindu, it is not true, at least nowadays, that every caste is a Hindu caste. There are also castes among the Mohammedans of India and they can also be found among the Buddhists. Even the Indian Christians have not been able wholly to avoid a recognition of the caste order . . . 'Caste' is, and remains, essentially social rank, and the central position of the Brahmans in Hinduism rests primarily upon the fact that social rank depends on the relationship to Brahmans . . .

So long as a tribe has not become a guest or a pariah people, it normally has a fixed territory. A proper caste never has such a territory. Usually in each village there is, or was, only one caste with a full title to the soil, but dependent village artisans and labourers also live there. The caste does not form a local, territorial, corporate body . . . A tribe is, or at least originally was, bound by obligations of blood revenge, whereas a caste never has anything to do with this custom.

A tribe normally comprises many, often almost all, of the occupations necessary for its subsistence. A caste may comprise people who follow very different pursuits; but the kinds of work permissible without a loss of caste membership are always strictly limited. Even today 'caste' and 'a way of earning a living' are so firmly linked that often a change of occupation is correlated with a split within a caste, which is not the case in a 'tribe' . . .

A tribe is originally and normally a political unit, which is either independent (as is always originally the case), or constitutes a part of a tribal league or of a political association (as in Greece) endowed with certain political tasks and having certain rights . . . A caste is never a political formation . . . By its very nature the caste is always a purely social and possibly occupational community . . .

Neither necessarily nor regularly does it form part of only one political formation, as it often spreads beyond . . . political boundaries.

The Caste and the Guild

. . . Guilds of merchants and craft guilds existed in India during the period of the development of cities and especially during the period of emergence of the great religions of salvation. During the period of the flowering of the cities, the position of the guilds in India could be compared to that of the guilds in the medieval Occident.

The association of guilds (the *mahajan*, literally the same as Italian *popolo grasso*, fat or big people) faced the prince on the one hand and on the other the economically dependent artisans. Their relations resembled those of the great guilds of the men of pen* and of merchants to the lower craft guilds (*popolo minuto*) of the Occident. There were also associations of lower craft guilds (the *panch*). Moreover, the servile guild of the Egyptian and late Roman kind was perhaps not entirely absent from the emerging patrimonial states of India. The distinctiveness of India lay in the fact that these beginnings of guild organisation in the cities led neither to city autonomy of the Occidental type nor to the social and economic organisation of the great patrimonial states of the Occident. Instead, the Hindu caste system, whose beginnings certainly preceded these organisations, smothered them.

. . . The merchant and craft guilds of the Occident had religious functions like those of the castes, which also involved questions of rank. The rank order which the guilds followed, in the processions, for instance, was a question which sometimes led to more bitter quarrels than did the clash of economic interests. Furthermore, in a 'closed' guild, that is, one with a fixed entry quota, the position of the master was hereditary. There were also quasi-guilds and associations derived from guilds in which the right to

---

* Presumably Weber refers to the lawyers.

membership was acquired through inheritance. In late Antiquity membership in the regimented guilds was compulsory and hereditary like the peasants' bondage to the soil. Furthermore, in the medieval Occident there were 'opprobrious' trades, which were religiously degrading and corresponded to the 'unclean' castes of India. None the less, the fundamental difference between occupational associations and caste remains . . . namely, the magical distance between the castes in their mutual relationships . . .

The positions of pariah peoples and pariah workers elsewhere (for example, the knacker and hangman) offered sociological analogies to the unclean castes of India. But although there were factual barriers restricting intermarriage between occupations of different status, there were no ritual barriers, which belong to the essence of the caste order . . . The hereditary character of the caste is not merely the result of monopolising occupations and restricting entry by a quota, as was the case among the closed guilds of the Occident which, in any case, were not at any time the most common form . . . The guild of the Occident, at least during the Middle Ages, allowed the apprentice to choose a master, thus making it possible for people to enter occupations other than those of their parents which never occurs in the caste system . . . Whereas the closure of the guilds became stricter with diminishing opportunities for making a living, among the castes the reverse was often observed, as they maintained their ritually prescribed way of life, and hence their inherited trade, most easily when economic opportunities were ample.

Another difference between guild and caste is of even greater importance. The occupational associations of the medieval Occident often fought one another but at the same time they tended to fraternise . . . No matter what the legal form was, the late medieval city in fact rested upon the fraternisation of its productive citizens . . . As a rule the fraternisation of the medieval citizenry was carried through by the fraternisation of the guilds while the roots of the ancient *polis* lay in the fraternisation of military associations which stemmed from clans. Every foundation of the Occidental city, in Antiquity and the Middle Ages, went together with the establishment of a cultic community. The common meal of the Greek dignitaries, the drinking rooms of the merchant and craft guilds, and their common processions to the church played a great role in Occidental cities. The caste order precluded this . . . If the member of a low caste merely looks at the meal of a Brahman he ritually defiles the Brahman . . . A separate lower caste (the Kallars) has arisen in Bengal from people who broke the ritual and dietary laws during the famine of 1866, and in consequence were excommunicated . . . At the time of the famine the pure castes were not satisfied with cleansing the defilement by penance. They succeeded in securing employment only of high-caste cooks whose hands were considered ritually clean by all the castes concerned. Furthermore, often fictitious walls were created between castes by means of chalk lines drawn around the tables . . .

By its solidarity, the association of Indian guilds, the *mahajan*, was a force with which the princes had to reckon . . . The guilds acquired privileges from the princes in exchange for loans – which is reminiscent of our medieval conditions. The elders of the guilds counted among the mightiest notables and ranked with the nobility and the priests. Where and when these conditions prevailed, the caste order was undeveloped and partly hindered and shaken by the religions of salvation, hostile to the Brahmans. The later transition to the rule of the caste system increased the power of the Brahmans and the princes, broke the power of the guilds and excluded fraternisation of the citizenry and of the trades. The prince could play off the castes against one another . . . This shift steered India's social structure – which appears to have stood for a time close to the threshold of European urban development – into a course that led far away from any such possibility . . .

The Peculiarities of the Caste Order

The Occident has known legally closed 'estates', but as a rule the bar against marrying outsiders held only to the extent that marriages contracted in spite of the rule constituted *mésalliances*, with the consequence that children acquired the status of the lower-ranking parent. Among the Hindus intermarriage between castes is prohibited while even intermarriage between subcastes is usually shunned. Even in the early books of law mixed bloods from different castes are assigned to a lower caste than either of the parents, and cannot belong to the three higher ('twice-born') castes. In earlier times intermarriage was absolutely excluded with the exception of hypergamy – a marriage of a man of higher rank to a woman of a lower, which was common. Marriage between a girl of higher caste and a lower-caste man was considered an offence against the honour of the girl's family. But to have a wife of lower caste was not considered an offence, and her children were not considered degraded, or only partially so. According to the law of inheritance, which is certainly the product of a later period, such children had to take second place in inheritance. Likewise the Israelite principle that the 'children of the servant' – and of the foreign woman – 'should not inherit in Israel' became the law in the later period.

The interest of upper-class men in the legality of polygamy, which they could afford, remained even when the acute shortage of women among the invading warriors had ended. The result was that the lower-caste girls had a large marriage market, and the lower the caste stood, the larger was their marriage market; whereas the marriage market for girls of the highest castes was restricted to their own caste . . . And this caused the women in the lower castes, by virtue of the general demand for women, to fetch high prices as brides. It was in part as a consequence of this dearth of women (in the lower castes) that polyandry originated. The formation of marriage cartels among villages or merchant castes in Gujarat and among peasant castes was a counter-measure against the hypergamy of the wealthy which raised the price of brides . . .

Among the upper castes, however, to find a bridegroom of high rank was difficult, and the more difficult it became, the more failure to marry was considered a disgrace for both the girl and her parents. The bridegroom had to be rewarded by the parents with an incredibly high dowry, and to find one (through professional match-makers) became the parents' most important worry, even during the infancy of the girl. Eventually it came to be considered an outright 'sin' for a girl to reach puberty without being married. This has led to grotesque results: the Kulin Brahmans are much in demand as bridegrooms; they have made a business of marrying *in absentia*, and for money, girls who remain with their families and see the bridegroom only if business or other reasons accidentally bring him where he has one of his 'wives' in residence. He shows his marriage contract to the father-in-law and uses his house as a 'cheap hotel', where without any costs he has the enjoyment of the girl who is considered his 'legitimate' wife.

Elsewhere infanticide is usually a result of the difficulties of subsistence among poor populations. But in India female infanticide was instituted by the upper castes, especially among the Rajputs. Despite the severe English laws of 1829, as late as 1869 in twenty-two villages of Rajputana there were 23 girls as against 284 boys. In an 1836 count, in one Rajput area, not one single live girl of over 1 year of age was found in a population of 10,000 souls! Infanticide existed alongside child marriage, in consequence of which some girls between 5 and 10 years old are already widowed and remain widowed for life. In India, as elsewhere, widow celibacy was added to widow suicide which was derived from the custom of the knight: the burial of his personal belongings, especially his women, with the dead lord . . .

In the southern states of America social intercourse between a white and a negro would result in a boycott of the former. The caste order enhances and transposes such an exclusion into the sphere of religion, or rather of magic. The Hindu dietary rules by no means concern merely the questions of (1) what may be eaten, and (2) who may eat at the same table. These two points are governed by strict rules, which confine these functions to members of the same caste. The dietary rules also regulate the further question (3) out of whose hand may one take food of a certain kind? For genteel houses this means, in the first place: whom may one use as a cook? Another question is (4) who is to be prevented from glancing at the food? . . . The caste order is religiously and ritually oriented to a degree not even partially attained elsewhere. Although the expression 'church' is not applicable to Hinduism, one can perhaps speak of a rank order of ecclesiastical estates.

When the census of India (1901) attempted to list by rank contemporary Hindu castes (two to three thousand or even more, according to the method of counting) . . . it distinguished the following groups. First, the Brahmans, and then the castes which claim, rightly or wrongly, to belong to the two other 'twice-born' castes of classical theory: the Kshatriya and the Vaishya.* They claim the right to wear the 'holy belt'. A third group of castes follows, the Shudra, the 'clean Shudra' of classical doctrine who may give water to a Brahman and from whose water bottle the Brahman accepts water. Close to them are the castes in northern and central India whose water a Brahman does not always accept (acceptance or non-acceptance depending on the Brahman's rank) or whose water he never accepts. The high-caste barber does not offer them all his services such as pedicure, and the laundryman does not wash their laundry. But they are not considered ritually 'unclean'. Finally, there are the castes regarded as unclean. All temples are closed to them, and no Brahman or barber will serve them. They must live outside the village district, and their touch (and, in southern India, even their presence at a distance of up to 64 feet) is regarded as polluting. All such restrictions are applied to castes which, according to the classical doctrine, originated from ritually forbidden sexual intercourse between members of different castes.

. . . Within these groupings one can find further gradations but these present extremely varied characteristics: among the upper castes the criterion is the correctness of practices concerning kinship, endogamy, child marriage, widow celibacy, cremation of the dead, ancestral sacrifice, foods and drink, and contacts with unclean castes. Among the lower castes one would have to differentiate according to the rank of the Brahmans who are still ready to serve them or who will not do so, and according to whether or not castes

---

* In the idealised original scheme the Kshatiyas were supposed to be warriors; the Vaishyas, merchants; the Shudras, peasants. (S.A.)

other than Brahmans accept water from them. The extraordinary variety of such rules forbids any more detailed treatment here . . .

The census workers had to face the problem: which unit should be considered as a caste? Within a group considered to be a caste there is neither necessarily intermarriage nor always full commensalism.* The subcaste is the predominantly endogamous unit, and in some castes there are several hundred subcastes. The subcastes are either purely local (diffused over districts of varying size), and/or they are delimited by actual or alleged descent, former or present occupation, or other differences in their style of life. Only the subcastes live under unified regulation, and they alone are organised – in so far as a caste organisation exists . . .

The sanctions against marriage and commensalism outside the caste are stronger than those against such relations between members of different subcastes within the same caste. Moreover, just as new subcastes form themselves easily, so the barriers between them are more unstable; whereas the barriers between castes are maintained with extraordinary perseverance.

It is perhaps impossible to ascertain the rank order of the castes, as it is contested and subject to change. An attempt was made in 1901 by the British census to settle this question but . . . it was not repeated as the excitement and discontent that resulted were out of all proportion to the value of the result. The attempt to classify the castes set off competing claims and the procurement of historical 'proofs' to support them . . .

The Political System and the Economy

In the Middle Ages elements of a truly feudal structure existed in most parts of India, particularly in the west – often in quite Occidental form. The rajas had coats of arms. There were enfeoffments with knightly ceremonies. But the books of law record no true seignorial rights in the villages.

* Eating together. (S.A.)

... The army of the epics and of the oldest historical sources (Megasthenes and Arrian) was similar to the Homeric army, although it represented a more advanced stage. The leaders of army divisions were not 'officers' but warriors distinguished by charismatic heroism. Combat took place without organisation, the heroes rushing to attack the most worthy opponents as at the time of the epics the death of the leader automatically signified the defeat of his army. [Later] there appeared warriors who could not equip themselves with weapons and chariots, and who received their pay from the prince and ranked below the nobles and priests, although they were separated from the peasants. In addition to organisation by phratries, as is found in Homer, there now appeared purely tactical divisions of ten, a hundred, or a thousand men in addition to elephants and chariots, cavalry and infantry. The armed forces were soon rationally organised, commanded by officers, and supplied and equipped increasingly out of royal stores. The army quickly lost all characteristics of a people's militia or a knights' host.

Royal administration developed a regulated hierarchical order of officials with local and functional spheres of authority; but administrative and court offices were not kept separate, and the jurisdictional spheres of a bewildering variety of offices were fluid, indeterminate, irrational and subject to chance influences.

As the inscriptions show, an elaborate filing system was devised as early as the first dynasty of great kings (that of the Maurya, in the third and fourth centuries BC) ... All inhabitants were registered by caste, clan, occupation, possessions and income, ... required to have passports and supervised throughout their lives. To fiscal authorities, the greatest danger to the state, next to subversion, was a weakening of the 'will to work'; and so theatres, musical bands, the alcohol trade and inns were subject to various restrictions. The spies of the government reported upon the most intimate details of private life of the subjects.

The king took part in trade, and government's market police controlled prices ... All conceivable sources of revenue were tapped: from taxes on prostitutes whom the king kept for travelling merchants, to fines on burghers whom the king would incite to commit punishable offences by means of *agents provocateurs*. In contrast to Buddhist and other pious sectarian kings, Hindu kings were interested only in the raising of manpower for the army and in tax collection . . .

The use of money developed in India at about the time of the growth of trade with the Hellenistic world, although overseas and caravan trade with Babylon and subsequently Egypt existed much earlier. In India, as in Babylon, the issuing of coined money, that is, money in some way signed, later stamped, or moulded metal blocks of a certain weight, remained at first a private business of the great trading families with a trustworthy seal. Silver, the metal of India's contempoary currency, was not mined in India. Gold, which the great kings of the early centuries used for coins, was produced only in small amounts. The treasures of precious metal were acquired through trade with the West and can be estimated from the accounts of the booty taken by the Mohammedans. These treasures were mainly hoarded although it was perhaps not accidental that one of the periods of flowering or renaissance of guild power during the second century AD coincided with the great influx of money from the Roman Empire. The rulers of the Maurya dynasty, including Ashoka, did not as yet mint coins of their own. The influx of precious metals from Greece and Rome stimulated the great kings of the first century AD to do so, but the old private coins and substitutes remained in circulation for a long time.

In India, as in Babylon, the lack of a state coinage did not hinder the rise of capitalist trade and political capitalism. From around the seventh century BC – for almost a thousand-year period – capitalism developed and expanded. The market appeared, and became the centre of administration. The cities lost their initial character as castles of the prince . . .

In the trading city are found most of the bazaars, workshops and homes of the *yavana* (Occidental) merchants. The luxury crafts are located in the royal city where the Brahmans, doctors, astrologers, bards, actors, musicians, flower-decorators, pearl string-makers and absentee landlords live. Between the two cities there is the market. The Tamil kings kept Roman mercenaries. Rich nobles moved into the cities to live on their rents. Accumulation of wealth through trade as well as rent became possible. Caravan trade was typically organised by caravan leaders, while the guilds rivalled the knights and priests in power. The king became financially dependent on the guilds and could only play them off against one another or bribe them. The merchants financed the wars of the princes who had to mortgage or lease rights and privileges to them as individuals or to their guild.

The rising patrimonial prince, with his disciplined army and officialdom, found the power of the guilds and his financial dependence on them increasingly unacceptable. We read that a *vanik* (trader) denied a war loan to a king, commenting that the duty of the prince was not to wage war but to protect peace and prosperity of the citizens. He added, however, that the loan could perhaps be given if the king could provide a suitable castle as security. There is described, furthermore, the king's great rage at a banquet when the trader castes refused to take their place among the Shudras, where the lord chamberlain had directed them, and left, protesting. He degraded these castes below the Shudras.

The opposition of the royal officials to the power of the plutocrats was natural. Kautilya's *Arthasastra** supplies evidence for this in the punishment of the goldsmiths who may have been engaged in the ancient practice of coinage, and who were money-lenders to princes. Added to their numerical weakness, certain peculiarly Indian conditions had fateful consequences for the bourgeoisie in their struggle against the patrimonial prince: the first was the absolute pacifism of the religions of salvation, Jainism and Buddhism, which were spreading at the time of the development of the cities; the second was the not yet fully developed but already established caste system. Both these factors blocked the development of the military power of the

---

* The title means the art of ruling, and the author is often described as the Indian Machiavelli.

citizenry - pacifism blocked it in principle, and the caste system did so by hindering the establishment of a city-state or *commune* in the European sense.

As far as we know, no republican city administration in the Occidental style developed in a lasting and proper form, despite early movements in this direction. In most Indian cities the king and his staff have always remained dominant, no matter what concessions they may have made in some cases to the power of the guilds. As a rule, guild power remained based purely on money without being backed by an independent military organisation. Hence it collapsed as soon as the princes found it expedient to rely upon priests and officials.

As in other parts of the world, the power of capital was great wherever numerous petty princes sought its support. In the long run, however, capital could not retain independent power in the face of the large empires.

The Brahmans and the kings used the intrinsically stronger caste organisation against the guilds. The caste could punish recalcitrant members with excommunication: as we know, sacerdotal means of coercion were also of paramount significance for the economic history of our Middle Ages. To secure observance of its rules (for example, to restrain competition among its members belonging to different castes), the guild could only request the castes to employ their sanctions or ask the king to intervene. After the defeat of the guilds the kings often commissioned traders as royal merchants with extensive monopolies of a mercantilist kind, investing them with high rank in a fashion quite similar to that recorded in modern Occidental history. However, the ancient independence of the guilds, and their role as representatives of the citizenry dealing with the king, had gone.

... Four types of craftsman appear in the Indian economic order from the epics until the Middle Ages and, in part, until the present. These are:

(1) Helots of single villages settled on the village outskirts who receive a fixed wage in kind or are given some land. The work of these artisans nearly always takes the

form of pure paid labour, the patron furnishing all the materials (helot handicraft).
(2) Artisans settled in their own separate, self-governing villages where they offer for sale their services or wares made from their own raw materials or sell their products personally or through traders on distant markets. They may also work at the homes of their patrons (tribal handicraft).
(3) Artisans settled by a king, prince, temple, or landlord on their lands. Such artisans can be either bondsmen or free but are in any case subject to compulsory labour and the obligation to supply the goods needed by the lord. They may combine this with price labour. Since the rise of patrimonialism such organisation of the crafts is represented primarily by defence workers, such as ship-builders and armorers who, reportedly, are often forbidden to work for private patrons. Blacksmiths and similar craftsmen are also subject to especially strict controls.
(4) Independent artisans settled in definite streets of the city who as price workers or wage workers offer their wares or their services in a bazaar (bazaar handicraft). A considerable part of the group are probably not permanent urban residents but an offshoot of the second type. Even now we learn from Bombay that an artisan, when aged or prosperous enough, often retires from the city to his village.

... The princes, especially the rich rulers of the trading cities of south India and Ceylon, recruited artisans from afar for the construction of palaces and temples. The princes endowed such immigrant artisans with land in return for their service as construction workers and artist craftsmen ... These royal artisans enjoyed a high degree of personal security. Under the Maurya dynasty anyone who caused a severe injury to an artisan had to suffer capital punishment ... Royal and temple artisans constituted high-quality labour among the Indian crafts. Secure in their grants, they could afford the time to manufacture artistic products. Commarasvamy mentions without further references a vase in Delhi which was produced by three generations of a family of royal artisans.

Like merchant guilds, the guilds of price workers evolved towards hereditary membership; they controlled the nature of the work (holidays, worktime), and guaranteed the quality of the wares by means of fines and other sanctions. However, many craftsmen were dependent on the traders and their putting-out system. Artisan castes, at least the upper crust of the artisan-artists, had an elaborate system of apprenticeship. The father, grand-uncle, or elder brother took turns as teaching masters and after the completion of apprenticeship, as masters of the house to whom all earnings had to be surrendered.

... In general, the tools of the Indian artisans were technically so simple that many of them made them themselves. Among some handicrafts the tools were worshipped as quasi-fetishes and even now some castes pay honours to them in the Dasahra festival. This stereotyping of tools was one of the strongest handicaps to all technical development, paralleled in the fine arts by the stereotyping of models, and the rejection of all imitation of nature. In some building crafts, particularly in handicrafts working with sacred objects, elements of technical procedure (e.g. painting the eye of a sacred picture) assumed the character of a magically important ceremony which had to be performed in accordance with definite rules. Any change of technique often required – usually with negative results – consultation of an oracle.

With the overthrow of the guilds by the princes, incipient urban developments of the Occidental type were eliminated. Allying themselves with the Brahmans, the patrimonial princes, in tune with the continental nature of India, relied on the rural populations as sources for armies and taxes.

... Royal power helped the Brahmans to suppress the heterodox religions of salvation of the urban citizenry and to thwart the aspirations of the prominent merchant and craft guilds ...

As in the Occident, patrimonial bureaucracy did not hinder but promoted the hereditary closure of trades and guilds. Its policy was merely to substitute interlocal corporation for purely local monopolies of the cities. There could be no question of an alliance of the princes with the capitalists in order to increase their power against their external rivals because of the continental character of India and the overwhelming importance of the land tax which could be raised at will . . .

With the Brahmans' help royal patrimonialism successfully subdued the citizenry . . . Brahmanical theory served as an unequalled tool to tame the subjects through religion. Finally, invasion and domination by foreign conquerors strengthened the Brahmans' monopoly of power. The foreign conquerors divested the most important competitors of the Brahmans of all power because they regarded them as politically dangerous. Thus the knighthood and the remnants of urban guilds were demoted.

The power of the Brahmans, in contrast, grew during the rule of the conquerors. After a period of fanatical iconoclasm and Islamic propaganda, the conquerors reconciled themselves to the continued existence of the Hindu culture, as priestly power under foreign domination always serves as a refuge for the conquered and as a tool of domestication for the overlords.

Religion and Society

As a closed system, the caste order is a product of consistent Brahmanical thought and could never have prevailed without the pervasive influence of the Brahmans as house priests, predicants, 'father confessors', advisers in all life situations, and royal officials whose skill in writing brought them into increasing demand as the bureaucratic administration expanded.

Ancient Indian conditions provided the building stones for the caste system: the interethnic specialisation of labour, the development of innumerable guest and pariah peoples, the organisation of village crafts on the basis of hereditary artisan cotters, the monopoly of internal trade by guest traders, the small extent of urban development, and the flow of occupational specialisation into the channels of hereditary segregation and hereditary allocation of customers. Likewise the beginnings of the bondage of occupations imposed by the princes with the aim of enforcing labour dues and collecting taxes, and (as an even stronger factor) their interest in legitimising their rule and domesticating their subjects, encouraged an alliance with the Brahmans for the sake of the preservation and stabilisation of the established sacred order.

All these factors of development of the caste system operated singly elsewhere. Only in India, however, did they operate jointly with special Indian circumstances: a conquered territory where indelible, sharp, 'racial' contrasts were accentuated by differences in skin colour. More predominant than anywhere else was magical rejection of social contact with strangers. This helped to preserve the charisma of noble clans and established insurmountable barriers between alien subject tribes, guest and pariah peoples and their overlords, even after the final integration of guest and pariah peoples into the local economic community. Individual acceptance for apprenticeship, participation in market deals, or citizenship – all these phenomena of the West either failed to develop in the first place or were crushed under the weight first of ethnic and later of caste fetters . . .

This well-integrated, unique social system must have existed as a finished idea long before it conquered even the greater part of north India. The legitimation of the caste through a combination of the *karma* doctrine with Brahmanical theology – in its way a stroke of genius – is plainly a product of rational ethical thought rather than of some economic 'conditions'. Only the wedding of this idea with the social order through the promise of rebirth gave this order its irresistible power over the thoughts and hopes of the people and provided a firm framework for the religious and social integration of the various professional groups and pariah peoples.

Where religious support of the social order is lacking – as in the case of Indian Islam – the caste order can be assimilated externally but remains lifeless, adapted to stabilising status differences, to representing economic interests through the borrowed institution of caste councils, and to adjusting people in other ways to the constraints of the social environment, but it is devoid of the 'spirit' which comes from its roots.

We can now inquire into the effects of the caste system on the economy. It must be inferred rather than inductively ascertained that these effects were essentially negative. We can only formulate a few generalisations. The main point is that this order is, by its nature, completely traditionalistic and anti-rational in its effects. The basis for this, however, must not be sought in the wrong place.

Karl Marx has characterised the peculiar position of the artisan in the Indian village – his dependence upon fixed payment in kind instead of upon production for the market – as the reason for the specific 'stability' of the Asiatic peoples. Marx was right in this.

In addition to the ancient village artisan, however, there were the merchants and also the urban artisans who either worked for the market or were economically dependent upon merchant guilds, as in the Occident. India has always been predominantly a country of villages, but the beginnings of the cities were also modest in the Occident, especially inland, and the position of the urban market in India was regulated by the princes in many ways as 'mercantilistically' as in the European territorial states at the beginnings of modern times. In any case, in so far as social stratification is concerned, not only the position of the village artisan but also the caste order as a whole must be viewed as the factors of stability. One must not think of this chain of causes and effects as simple. One might believe, for instance, that mutual avoidance between ritual castes made impossible the development of 'large-scale enterprises' with a division of labour in the same workshop. But such is not the case.

The law of caste has proved just as elastic in the face of concentration of labour in workshops as it did in the face of a need for gathering labourers and servants in a noble household. All domestic servants required by the upper castes were ritually clean. The principle 'the artisan's hand is always clean in his work' is a similar concession to the need to have fixtures, repairs, or other work done, and personal services furnished, by wage or itinerant workers not belonging to the household. Likewise, the workshop was recognised as 'clean'. Hence no ritual factor would have stood in the way of employing different castes together in the same large workroom, just as the ban on interest during the Middle Ages did little to hinder the growth of profit-making capital, which anyway did not develop in the form of investment for fixed interest. The core of the obstacle did not lie in such particular difficulties, which every one of the great religious systems in its own manner placed, or seemed to place, in the way of the modern economy. The core of the obstruction was rather embedded in the 'spirit' of the whole system. Though not always easy, eventually it became possible in modern times to employ Indian caste labour in factories. And even earlier it was possible to use the labour of Indian artisans in capitalistic manner, as was usual in other colonial areas, after the complete mechanism of modern capitalism had been imported from Europe. Despite all this, it must still be considered extremely unlikely that the modern organisation of industrial capitalism would ever have *originated* on the basis of the caste system. A ritual law in which every change of occupation, every change in work technique, may result in ritual degradation is certainly not adapted to giving birth to economic and technical revolutions, or even to facilitating the first germination of capitalism in its midst. The inherently strong traditionalism of the artisan was inevitably heightened to the extreme by the caste order. Commercial capital, in its attempts to organise industrial labour on the basis of the putting-out system, had to face substantially stronger resistance in India than in the Occident. The traders themselves in their ritual seclusion remained in the shackles of the typical Oriental pattern which by itself has never created a modern capitalist organisation of labour. An analogous situation could arise elsewhere if only guest peoples, like the Jews, who were ritually exclusive towards one another and towards third parties, were to divide among themselves all the trades in one economic area . . .

According to doctrine the order and rank of the castes is as eternal as the courses of the stars and the difference between the animal species and the human races. To attempt to overthrow them would be senseless. Rebirth can drag man down into the life of a 'worm in the intestine of a dog', but, according to his conduct, it may raise and place him into the womb of a queen and Brahman's daughter. Absolute requirements, however, are strict fulfilment of caste obligations in the present life and the shunning of any sacrilegious attempt to move out of one's caste. A lasting devotion to one's calling is anchored in the Hindu promise of rebirth more firmly than in any other social ethic because Hinduism does not link it with teachings about the moral value of vocational stability and pious modesty, as did the patriarchal forms of Christendom, but with the individual's personal interest in salvation. Together with the dread of the magical consequences of innovation this places a high premium on loyalty to the caste. The doctrine of Hindu salvation promises rebirth as a king, noble, and so on (according to his present rank) to the artisan who in his work follows traditional prescriptions and never overcharges or deceives about the quality . . . The neglect of one's caste duties, prompted by high aspirations, unfailingly brings harm in the present or future life.

It is difficult to imagine a more traditionalistic conception of professional virtues than those of Hinduism. The castes might face one another with bitter hatred – for the idea that everybody merits his own fate does not make other people's good fortune more digestible for the unfortunate. However, so long as the *karma* doctrine remained unshaken, revolutionary ideas or progressivism were inconceivable, particularly as the lowest castes had most to gain through ritual correctness and were therefore least inclined towards innovation.

It was impossible to shatter this traditionalism, based on ritualism and anchored in the *karma* doctrine, and to rationalise the economy.

5

The Nature of Modern Capitalism

Capitalism is present wherever provision for the needs of a human group is carried out by private business. More specifically, a rational capitalistic establishment is one with capital accounting, that is, an establishment which ascertains its income-yielding assets, profits and costs by calculation according to the methods of modern book-keeping. The practice of balancing the books was first insisted upon by the Dutch theorist Simon Stevin in the year 1698.

While capitalism of various forms can be found in all periods of history, the provision for the everyday wants by capitalistic methods is characteristic of the Occident alone and even here has been the predominant method only since the middle of the nineteenth century.

The most general presupposition for the existence of this capitalism is that of rational capital accounting. Such accounting involves, first, the appropriation of all physical means of production – land, raw materials, machinery, tools, and so on – as disposable property of autonomous private industrial enterprises. This is a phenomenon known only in our time, when the army alone forms a universal exception to it. In the second place, it involves freedom of the market, that is, the absence of irrational limitations on trading. Such limitations might be concerned with barriers of status, when a certain mode of life or consumption is prescribed for a class, as for example when the townsman was not allowed to own an estate or the knight or peasant to carry on industry. In such situations neither a free labour market nor a free commodity market can exist. Thirdly, capitalistic accounting presupposes rational technology.

The fourth requirement is that of calculable law. The

capitalistic form of industrial organisation, if it is to operate rationally, must be able to depend upon calculable adjudication and administration. Neither in the age of the Greek city-states nor in the patrimonial states of Asia nor in the Western European countries down to the Stuarts was this condition fulfilled. The royal 'cheap justice' with its remissions by royal grace introduced continual disturbances into the calculations of economic life.

The fifth requirement is free labour. People must be available who are not only legally in the position to do so but are also economically compelled to sell their labour on the market without restrictions. Only where in consequence of the existence of workers who in the formal sense voluntarily, but actually under the compulsion of hunger, offer themselves to work for a wage, can the costs of production be unambiguously determined in advance. The sixth and final condition is the commercialisation of economic life. By this we mean the general use of commercial instruments to represent share rights in an enterprise . . . when property takes on the form of negotiable paper.

6
Protestantism and the Spirit of Capitalism

What is to be understood by the *spirit* of capitalism? Such a historical concept, since it refers to a phenomenon significant for its unique individuality, cannot be defined according to the formula *genus proximum, differentia specifica*, but must be gradually put together out of the individual parts which are taken from historical reality. Thus the final and definitive concept cannot stand at the beginning of the investigation, but must come at the end.

. . . we turn to a document of that spirit which contains what we are looking for in almost classical purity, and at the same time has the advantage of being free from all direct relationship to religion, being thus, for our purposes, free of preconceptions.

> Remember, that *time* is money. He that can earn ten shillings a day by his labour, and goes abroad, or sits idle, one half of that day, though he spends but sixpence during his diversion or idleness, ought not to reckon *that* the only expense; he has really spent, or rather thrown away, five shillings besides.
>
> Remember, that *credit* is money. If a man lets his money lie in my hands after it is due, he gives me the interest, or so much as I can make of it during that time. This amounts to a considerable sum where a man has good and large credit, and makes good use of it.
>
> Remember, that money is of the prolific, generating nature. Money can beget money, and its offspring can beget more, and so on. Five shillings turned is six, turned

again it is seven and threepence, and so on, till it becomes a hundred pounds. The more there is of it, the more it produces every turning, so that the profits rise quicker and quicker. He that kills a breeding-sow, destroys all her offspring to the thousandth generation. He that murders a crown, destroys all that it might have produced, even scores of pounds.

Remember this saying, *The good paymaster is lord of another man's purse.* He that is known to pay punctually and exactly to the time he promises, may at any time, and on any occasion, raise all the money his friends can spare. This is sometimes of great use. After industry and frugality, nothing contributes more to the raising of a young man in the world than punctuality and justice in all his dealings; therefore never keep borrowed money an hour beyond the time you promised, lest a disappointment shut up your friend's purse for ever.

The most trifling actions that affect a man's credit are to be regarded. The sound of your hammer at five in the morning, or eight at night, heard by a creditor, makes him easy six months longer; but if he sees you at a billiard-table, or hears your voice at a tavern, when you should be at work, he sends for his money the next day; demands it, before he can receive it, in a lump.

It shows, besides, that you are mindful of what you owe; it makes you appear a careful as well as an honest man, and that still increases your credit.

Beware of thinking all your own that you possess, and of living accordingly. It is a mistake that many people who have credit fall into. To prevent this, keep an exact account for some time both of your expenses and your income. If you take the pains at first to mention particulars, it will have this good effect: you will discover how wonderfully small, trifling expenses mount up to large sums, and will discern what might have been, and may for the future be saved, without occasioning any great inconvenience.

For six pounds a year you may have the use of one

hundred pounds, provided you are a man of known prudence and honesty.

He that spends a groat a day idly, spends idly above six pounds a year, which is the price for the use of one hundred pounds.

He that wastes idly a groat's worth of his time per day, one day with another, wastes the privilege of using one hundred pounds each day.

He that idly loses five shillings' worth of time, loses five shillings, and might as prudently throw five shillings into the sea.

He that loses five shillings, not only loses that sum, but all the advantage that might be made by turning it in dealing, which by the time that a young man becomes old, will amount to a considerable sum of money.

It is Benjamin Franklin who preaches to us in these sentences. That it is the spirit of capitalism which here speaks in characteristic fashion, no one will doubt, however little we may wish to claim that everything which could be understood as pertaining to that spirit is contained in it. Let us pause a moment to consider this passage, the philosophy of which Kürnberger sums up in the words 'They make tallow out of cattle and money out of men'. The peculiarity of this philosophy of avarice appears to be the ideal of the honest man of recognised credit, and above all the idea of a duty of the individual towards the increase of his capital, which is assumed as an end in itself. Truly what is here preached is not simply a means of making one's way in the world, but a peculiar ethic. The infraction of its rules is treated not as foolishness but as forgetfulness of duty. That is the essence of the matter. It is not mere business astuteness – that sort of thing is common enough; it is an ethos. *This* is the quality which interests us.

When speaking to a business associate who had retired and who wanted to persuade him to do the same, on the ground that he had made enough money and should let others have a chance, Jacob Fugger rejected that as pusillanimity and answered that he thought otherwise and wanted to make money as long as he could, the spirit of his statement is evidently quite different from that of Franklin. What in Fugger's case was a morally neutral expression of commercial daring and personal inclination, for Franklin takes on the character of an ethically coloured maxim for the conduct of life.

All Franklin's moral attitudes are coloured with utilitarianism. Honesty is useful, because it assures credit; so are punctuality, industry and frugality, and that is the reason why they are virtues. A logical deduction from this would be that where, for instance, the appearance of honesty serves the same purpose, that would suffice, and an unnecessary surplus of this virtue would evidently appear to Franklin's eyes as unproductive waste. And as a matter of fact, the story in his autobiography of his conversion to those virtues, or the discussion of the value of a strict maintenance of the appearance of modesty, the assiduous belittlement of one's own deserts in order to gain general recognition later, confirm this impression. According to Franklin, those virtues, like all others, are only virtues in so far as they are actually useful to the individual, and the surrogate of mere appearance is always sufficient when it accomplishes the end in view. But in fact the matter is not by any means so simple. Benjamin Franklin's own character, as it appears in the really unusual candidness of his autobiography, belies that suspicion. The fact that he ascribes his recognition of the utility of virtue to a divine revelation which was intended to lead him in the path of righteousness shows that something more than mere garnishing for purely egocentric motives is involved.

Man is dominated by the making of money, by acquisition as the ultimate purpose of his life. Economic acquisition is no longer subordinated to man as the means for the satisfaction of his material needs. This reversal of what we should call the natural relationship, so irrational from a naïve point of view, is evidently as definitely a leading principle of capitalism as it is foreign to all peoples not under capitalistic influence. At the same time it expresses a type of feeling which is closely connected with certain religious ideas. If we thus ask, *why* should 'money be made out of men', Benjamin Franklin himself, although he was a colourless deist, answers in his autobiography with a quotation from the Bible, which his strict Calvinistic father drummed into him again and again in his youth: 'Seest thou a man diligent in his business? He shall stand before kings' (Proverbs 22: 29). The earning of money within the modern economic order is, so long as it is done legally, the result and the expression of virtue and proficiency in a calling; and this virtue and proficiency are, as it is now not difficult to see, the real alpha and omega of Franklin's ethic, as expressed in the passages we have quoted, as well as in all his works without exception.

In truth this peculiar idea, so familiar to us today, but in reality so little a matter of course, of one's duty in a calling, is what is most characteristic of the social ethic of capitalistic culture, and is in a sense the fundamental basis of it. It is an obligation which the individual is supposed to feel and does feel towards the content of his professional activity, no matter in what it consists, in particular no matter whether it appears on the surface as a utilisation of his personal powers, or only of his material possessions (as capital).

Of course, this conception has not appeared only under capitalistic conditions. On the contrary, we shall later trace its origin back to a time previous to the advent of capitalism. Still less, naturally, do we maintain that a conscious acceptance of these ethical maxims on the part of the individuals, entrepreneurs or labourers in modern capitalistic enterprises is a condition of the further existence of present-day capitalism. The capitalistic economy of the present day is an immense cosmos into which the individual is born, and which presents itself to him, at least as an individual, as an unalterable order of things in which he must live. It forces the individual, in so far as he is involved in the system of market relationships, to conform to capitalistic rules of action. The manufacturer who in the long run acts counter to these norms will be eliminated from the economic scene just as inevitably as the worker who cannot or will not adapt himself to them will be thrown into the street without a job.

Thus the capitalism of today, which has come to dominate economic life, educates and selects the economic subjects which it needs through a process of economic survival of the fittest. But here one can easily see the limits of the concept of selection as a means of historical explanation. In order that a manner of life so well adapted to the peculiarities of capitalism could be selected at all, that is, should come to dominate others, it had to originate somewhere, and not in isolated individuals alone, but as a way of life common to whole groups of men. This origin is what really needs explanation. Concerning the doctrine of the more naïve historical materialism, that such ideas originate as a reflection or superstructure of economic situations, we shall speak more in detail below. At this point it will suffice for our purpose to call attention to the fact that without doubt, in the place of Benjamin Franklin's birth (Massachusetts), the spirit of capitalism (in the sense we have attached to it) was present before the capitalistic order. There were complaints of a peculiarly calculating sort of profit-seeking in New England, as distinguished from other parts of America, as early as 1632. It is further beyond doubt that capitalism remained far less developed in some of the neighbouring colonies, the later Southern States of the United States of America, in spite of the fact that these latter were founded by large capitalists for business motives, while the New England colonies were founded by preachers and seminary graduates with the help of petty bourgeois, craftsmen and yeomen, for religious reasons. In this case the causal relation is certainly the reverse of that suggested by the materialistic standpoint.

But the origin and history of such ideas is much more complex than the theorists of the superstructure suppose. The spirit of capitalism, in the sense in which we are using the term, had to fight its way to supremacy against a whole world of hostile forces. A state of mind such as that expressed in the passages we have quoted from Franklin, which called forth the applause of a whole people, would both in ancient times and in the Middle Ages have been proscribed as the lowest sort of avarice and as an attitude entirely lacking in self-respect. It is, in fact, still regularly thus looked upon by all those social groups which are least involved in or adapted to modern capitalistic conditions. This is not wholly because the instinct of acquisition was in those times unknown or undeveloped, as has often been said. Nor was it because the greed for gold was then, or is now, less powerful outside bourgeois capitalism than within its peculiar sphere, as the illusions of modern romanticists would lead us to believe. The difference between the capitalistic and pre-capitalistic spirit is not to be found at this point. The greed of the Chinese mandarin, the old Roman aristocrat, or the modern peasant can stand up to any comparison. And the hunger for money of a Neapolitan cab-driver or of Asiatic representatives of similar trades, as well as of the craftsmen of southern European or Asiatic countries, is, as anyone can find out for himself, very much more intense, and especially more unscrupulous, than that of, say, an Englishman in similar circumstances.

The universal reign of absolute unscrupulousness in the pursuit of selfish interests by the making of money has been a specific characteristic of precisely those countries whose bourgeois-capitalistic development, measured according to Occidental standards, has remained backward. At all periods of history, wherever it was possible, there has been ruthless acquisition, bound by no ethical norms whatever. Like war and piracy, trade has often been unrestrained in its relations with foreigners and those outside the group. The double ethic has permitted here what was forbidden in dealings among brothers.

Capitalistic acquisition as an adventure has been at home in all types of economic society which have known trade with the use of money and which have offered it opportunities, through accepting goods for sale with commission, farming of taxes, state loans, the financing of wars, ducal courts and office-holders. Likewise the inner attitude of the adventurer, who laughs at all ethical limitations, has been universal. Absolute and conscious ruthlessness in acquisition has often stood in the closest connection with the strictest conformity to tradition.

The most important opponent with which the spirit of capitalism, in the sense of a definite concept of life claiming ethical sanction, has had to struggle, was that type of attitude and reaction to new situations which we may designate as traditionalism. In this case also every attempt at a final definition must be held in abeyance. On the other hand, we must try to make the provisional meaning clear by citing a few cases. We will begin from below, with the labourers.

One of the technical means which the modern employer uses in order to secure the greatest possible amount of work from his men is the device of piece-rates. In agriculture, for instance, the gathering of the harvest is a case where the greatest possible intensity of labour is called for, since, the weather being uncertain, the difference between high profit and heavy loss may depend on the speed with which the harvesting can be done. Hence a system of piece-rates is almost universal here. And attempts have again and again been made, by increasing the piece-rates of the workmen, thereby giving them an opportunity to earn what is for them a very high wage, to interest them in increasing their own efficiency. But a peculiar difficulty has been met with surprising frequency: raising the piece-rates has often had the result that not more but less has been accomplished in the same time, because the worker has reacted to the increase not by increasing but by decreasing the amount of his work. For instance, a man who at the rate of 1 mark per acre mowed $2\frac{1}{2}$ acres per day and earned $2\frac{1}{2}$ marks, when the rate was raised to 1·25 marks per acre mowed, not 3 acres, as he might easily have done, thus earning 3·75 marks, but only 2 acres, so that he could still earn the $2\frac{1}{2}$ marks to which he was accustomed. The opportunity of earning more was less attractive than that of working less. He did not ask: how much can I earn in a day if I do as much work as possible? but: how much must I work in order to earn the wage, $2\frac{1}{2}$ marks, which I earned before and which takes care of my traditional needs? This is an example of what is here meant by traditionalism. A man does not 'by nature' wish to earn more and more money, but simply to live as he is accustomed to live and to earn as much as is necessary for that purpose. Wherever modern capitalism has begun its work of increasing the productivity of human labour by increasing its intensity, it has encountered the immensely stubborn resistance of this leading trait of pre-capitalistic labour. And today it encounters it the more, the more backward (from a capitalistic point of view) the labouring forces are with which it has to deal.

The capitalistic form of an enterprise and the spirit in which it is run generally stand in some sort of relationship of adequacy to each other, but not in one of necessary interdependence. Nevertheless, we provisionally use the expression 'spirit of (modern) capitalism' to describe that attitude which seeks profit rationally and systematically in the manner which we have illustrated by the example of Benjamin Franklin. This, however, is justified by the historical fact that that attitude of mind has on the one hand found its most suitable expression in capitalistic enterprise, while on the other the enterprise has derived its most suitable motive force from the spirit of capitalism.

But the two may very well occur separately. Benjamin Franklin was filled with the spirit of capitalism at a time when his printing business did not differ in form from any handicraft enterprise. And we shall see that at the beginning of modern times it was by no means the capitalistic entrepreneurs of the commercial aristocracy who were either the sole or the predominant bearers of the attitude we have here called the spirit of capitalism. It was much more the rising strata of the lower industrial middle classes. Even in the nineteenth century its classical representatives were not the elegant gentlemen of Liverpool and Hamburg, with their commercial fortunes handed down for generations, but the self-made men of Manchester and Westphalia, who often rose from very modest circumstances. As early as the sixteenth century the situation was similar; the industries which arose at that time were mostly created by self-made men.

The management, for instance, of a bank, a wholesale export business, a large retail establishment, or of a large putting-out enterprise dealing with goods produced in homes, is certainly only possible in the form of a capitalistic enterprise. Nevertheless, they may all be carried on in a traditionalistic spirit. In fact, the business of a large bank of issue cannot be carried on in any other way. The foreign trade of whole epochs has rested on the basis of monopolies and legal privileges of strictly traditional character. In retail trade – and we are not here talking of the small men without capital who are continually crying out for government aid – the revolution which is making an end of the old traditionalism is still in full swing. It is the same development which broke up the old putting-out system, to which modern domestic labour is related only in form. How this revolution takes place and what is its significance may, in spite of the fact these things are so familiar, be again brought out by a concrete example.

Until about the middle of the last century the life of a putter-out was, at least in many of the branches of the Continental textile industry, what we should today consider very comfortable. We may imagine its routine somewhat as follows. The peasants came with their cloth, often (in the case of linen) principally or entirely made from raw material which the peasant himself had produced, to the town in which the putter-out lived, and after a careful, often official, appraisal of the quality, received the customary price for it. The putter-out's customers, for markets any appreciable distance away, were middlemen, who also came to him, generally not yet following the fashion, but seeking traditional qualities, and bought from his warehouse, or, long before delivery, placed orders which were probably in turn passed on to the peasants. Personal canvassing of customers took place, if at all, only at long intervals. Otherwise correspondence sufficed, though the sending of samples slowly gained ground. The number of business hours was very moderate, perhaps five to six a day, sometimes considerably less; more in the rush season, where there was one. Earnings were moderate; enough to lead a respectable life and in good times to put away a little. On the whole, relations among competitors were relatively good, with a large degree of agreement on the fundamentals of business. A long daily visit to the tavern, often with plenty to drink, and a congenial circle of friends made life comfortable and leisurely.

The form of organisation was in every respect capitalistic; the entrepreneur's activity was of a purely business character; the use of capital, turned over in the business, was indispensable; and finally, the objective aspect of the economic process, the book-keeping, was rational. But it was traditionalistic business, if one considers the spirit which animated the entrepreneur: the traditional manner of life, the traditional rate of profit, the traditional amount of work, the traditional manner of regulating the relationships with labour, and the essentially traditional circle of customers and the manner of attracting new ones. All these dominated the conduct of the business, were at the basis, one may say, of the ethos of this group of businessmen.

Now at some time this leisureliness was suddenly destroyed, and often entirely without any essential change in the form of organisation, such as the transition to a unified factory, to mechanical weaving, and so on. What happened was, on the contrary, often no more than this: some young man from one of the putting-out families went out into the country, carefully chose weavers for his employ, greatly increased the rigour of his supervision of their work, and thus turned them from peasants into labourers. On the other hand, he would begin to change his marketing methods by as far as possible going directly to the final customer, would take the details into his own hands, would personally solicit customers, visiting them every year, and above all would adapt the quality of the product directly to their needs and wishes. At the same time he began to introduce the principle of low prices and large turnover. There was repeated what everywhere and always is the result of such a process of rationalisation: those who would not follow suit had to go out of business. The idyllic state collapsed under the pressure of a bitter competitive struggle, respectable fortunes were made, and not lent out at interest, but always reinvested in the business. The old leisurely and comfortable attitude towards life gave way to a hard frugality in which some participated and came to the top, because they did not wish to consume but to earn, while others who wished to keep on with the old ways were forced to curtail their consumption.

And, what is most important in this connection, it was not generally in such cases a stream of new money invested in the industry which brought about this revolution – in several cases known to me the whole revolutionary process was set in motion with a capital of a few thousands borrowed from relations – but the new spirit, the spirit of modern capitalism, which had set to work. The question of the motive forces in the expansion of modern capitalism is not in the first instance a question of the origin of the capital sums which were available for capitalistic uses but, above all, of the development of the spirit of capitalism. Where it appears and is able to work itself out, it produces its own capital and monetary supplies as the means to its ends; but the reverse is not true. Its entry on the scene was not generally peaceful. A flood of mistrust, sometimes of hatred, above all of moral indignation, regularly opposed itself to the first innovator. Often – I know of several cases of the sort – regular legends of mysterious shady spots earlier in his life have been produced. It is very easy not to recognise that only an unusually strong character could save an entrepreneur of this new type from the loss of his temperate self-control and from both moral and economic shipwreck. Furthermore, along with clarity of vision and ability to act, it is only by virtue of very definite and highly developed ethical qualities that it has been possible for him to command the absolutely indispensable confidence of his customers and workmen. Nothing else could have given him the strength to overcome the innumerable obstacles, above all the infinitely more intensive work which is demanded of the modern entrepreneur. But these are ethical qualities of quite a different sort from those adapted to the traditionalism of the past.

And, as a rule, it has been neither dare-devil and unscrupulous speculators – economic adventurers such as we meet at all periods of economic history – nor simply great financiers who have carried through this change, outwardly so inconspicuous, but nevertheless so decisive for the penetration of economic life with the new spirit. On the contrary, they have been men who have grown up in the hard school of life, calculating and daring at the same time, above all temperate and reliable, shrewd and completely devoted to their business, with strictly bourgeois opinions and principles.

Of course, the desire for the power and recognition which the mere fact of wealth brings plays its part. The ideal type of the capitalistic entrepreneur avoids ostentation and unnecessary expenditure, as well as conscious enjoyment of his power, and is embarrassed by the outward signs of social recognition which he receives. His manner of life is distinguished by a certain ascetic tendency, as appears clearly enough in the sermon of Franklin which we have quoted. That is to say it is by no means exceptional, but rather the rule, for him to have a sort of modesty which is essentially more honest than the reserve which Franklin so shrewdly recommends. He gets nothing out of his wealth for himself, except the irrational sense of having done his job well.

But it is just that which seems to the pre-capitalistic man so incomprehensible and mysterious, so unworthy and contemptible. That anyone should be able to make it the sole purpose of his life-work to sink into the grave weighed down with a great material load of money and goods seems to him explicable only as the product of a perverse instinct, the hunger for money.

At present under our individualistic political, legal and economic institutions, with the forms of organisation and general structure which are peculiar to our economic order, this spirit of capitalism might be understandable, as has been said, purely as a result of adaptation. The capitalistic system demands this devotion to the calling of making money – an attitude towards material goods which is so well suited to that system and so intimately bound up with the conditions of survival in the economic struggle for existence that there can today no longer be any question of a necessary connection of that acquisitive manner of life with any particular view of the world. In fact, it no longer needs the support of any religious forces, and feels the attempts of religion to influence economic life, in so far as they can still be felt at all, to be as much an unjustified interference as its regulation by the state. In such circumstances men's commercial and social interests tend to determine their opinions and attitudes. Whoever does not adapt his manner of life to the conditions of capitalistic success must go under, or at least cannot rise. These are phenomena of a time in which modern capitalism has become dominant and has become emancipated from its old supports. At one time it was able to destroy the old forms of medieval regulation of economic life only in alliance with the growing power of the modern state, and the same can be said about its relations with religious forces. The conception of money-making as an end in itself to which people were bound, as a calling, was contrary to the ethical feelings of whole epochs. St Thomas's characterisation of the desire for gain as turpitude (which term even included unavoidable and hence ethically justified profit-making) already contained a high degree of concession on the part of the Catholic doctrine to the financial powers with which the church had such intimate political relations in the Italian cities, as compared with the much more radically anti-chrematistic* views of wider circles. The dominant doctrine rejected the spirit of capitalistic acquisition as turpitude or at least could not give it a positive ethical sanction. An ethical attitude like that of Benjamin Franklin would have been simply unthinkable. This was, above all, the attitude of capitalistic circles themselves. Their life-work was, so long as they clung to the tradition of the church, at best something morally indifferent. It was tolerated, but was still, even if only on account of the continual danger of collision with the church's doctrine on usury, somewhat dangerous to salvation. Quite considerable sums, as the sources show, went at the death of rich people to religious institutions as conscience money, at times even back to former debtors as proceeds of usury which had been unjustly taken from them. It was otherwise, along with heretical and other tendencies, looked upon with disapproval only in those parts of the commercial aristocracy which were already emancipated from the tradition. But even sceptics and people indifferent to the church often reconciled themselves with it by gifts, because it was a sort of insurance against the uncertainties of what might come after death.

How could activity, which was at best ethically tolerated, turn into a calling in the sense described by Benjamin Franklin? The fact to be explained historically is that in the

*'Anti-chrematistic' means against money-making. (S.A.)

most highly capitalistic centre of that time, in Florence of the fourteenth and fifteenth centuries, the money and capital market of all the great political powers, this attitude was considered ethically unjustifiable, or at best to be tolerated. But in the small towns in the backwoods of Pennsylvania in the eighteenth century, where because of simple lack of money business was in danger of sliding back into barter, where there was hardly a sign of large enterprise, where only the earliest beginnings of banking were to be found, the same activity was considered as essence of moral conduct, even commanded in the name of duty. To speak here of a reflection of material conditions in the ideal superstructure would be patent nonsense.

Work in the service of a rational organisation for the provision of humanity with material goods has without doubt always appeared to representatives of the capitalistic spirit as one of the most important purposes of their life. It is only necessary, for instance, to read Franklin's account of his efforts in the service of civic improvements in Philadelphia clearly to apprehend this obvious truth. And the joy and pride of having given employment to numerous people, of having had a part in the economic progress of his home town in the sense referring to figures of population and volume of trade which capitalism associated with the world, all these things obviously are part of the specific and undoubtedly idealistic satisfactions in life to modern men of business.

7
Religion and Other Factors in the Development of Modern Capitalism

It is a widespread error to regard the increase of population as a really crucial agent in the evolution of Western capitalism. The growth of population in the West made most rapid progress from the beginning of the eighteenth century to the end of the nineteenth. In the same period China experienced a population growth of at least equal extent – from 60 or 70 to 400 million. In spite of this fact, capitalism went backwards in China, not forward. The growth of population in Europe did indeed favour the development of capitalism in so far as in a small population the system would have been unable to secure the necessary labour force, but in itself it never called forth that development.

Nor can the inflow of precious metals be regarded, as Sombart suggests, as the primary cause of the advent of capitalism. It is certainly true that in a given situation an increase in the supply of precious metals may give rise to price revolutions, such as that which took place after 1530 in Europe, and progress may be stimulated by the fact that large amounts of cash come into the hands of certain groups. But the case of India proves that such an importation of precious metal will not alone bring forth capitalism. During the period of Roman power an enormous mass of precious metal . . . came into India in exchange for domestic goods, but this inflow gave rise to commercial capitalism only to a slight extent. The greater part of the precious metal disappeared in the hoards of the rajas instead of being converted into money and used for setting up enterprises of a rational capitalistic character. This fact proves that it depends entirely upon the nature of the economic system what will be the result of an inflow of precious metals. The gold and silver from America, after its discovery, flowed in the first place to Spain, but in that country capitalistic development went into reverse parallel with the importation. There followed, on the one hand, the suppression of the *communeros* and the destruction of commercial interests by the Spanish grandees, and, on the other hand, the employment of the money for military ends. Consequently, the stream of precious metal flowed through Spain, scarcely touching it, and fertilised other countries, which in the fifteenth century were already undergoing a process of transformation in relations of production which was favourable to capitalism.

Hence neither the growth of population nor the importation of precious metal has produced Western capitalism. The first pre-conditions for the development of capitalism were geographical. In China and India the enormous costs of transportation, connected with the decisively inland commerce of the regions, formed serious obstacles to making profits through trade and to using capital in the construction of a capitalistic system, while in the West the position of the Mediterranean as an inland sea, and the abundant interconnections through the rivers, favoured the development of international commerce. But this factor in its turn must not be overestimated. The civilisation of Antiquity was distinctively coastal. Here the opportunities for commerce were very favourable (because of the character of the Mediterranean Sea, in contrast to the Chinese waters with their typhoons), and yet no capitalism arose in Antiquity.* Moreover, in the modern period capitalistic development was much more intense in Florence than in Genoa or in Venice. Capitalism in the West was born in the industrial cities of the interior rather than in the cities that were centres of sea trade.

* This text was published posthumously from notes. Had he corrected it, Weber would have put 'fully developed' or 'rational' in front of 'capitalism' because elsewhere he says that there was capitalism in Antiquity but it was 'irrational', 'political', or 'booty capitalism'. The last two predicates make clearer what he had in mind. In the Introduction I have suggested that Weber's term 'rational' ought to be replaced as a characterisation of capitalism by 'industrial' or 'productive'.

... In the last analysis the factor which produced capitalism is the rational permanent enterprise, with its rational accounting, rational technology and rational law, but again not these alone. Necessary complementary factors were the rational spirit, the rationalisation of the conduct of life in general and a rationalistic economic ethic.

The earliest form of economic ethics, and of the economic relations which result from it, is the sanctity of tradition.

... Primitive traditionalism may undergo essential intensification through two circumstances. In the first place, material interests may be tied up with the maintenance of tradition. When, for example, in China an attempt was made to change certain roads or to introduce more rational means or routes of transportation, the perquisites of certain officials were threatened; and the same was the case in the Middle Ages in the West, and in modern times when railroads were introduced. Such vested interests of officials, landholders and merchants contributed decisively to stifling a tendency toward rationalisation. Stronger still is the stereotyping of business on magical grounds, stemming from a deep repugnance towards undertaking any change in the established conduct of life because supernatural evils are feared. Commonly a defence of some economic privilege is also involved, but its effectiveness depends on a general belief in the potency of the magical processes which are feared.

Such traditional obstructions cannot be overcome by the economic impulse alone. It is an erroneous notion that our rationalistic and capitalistic age is characterised by a stronger economic interest than other periods, since the moving spirits of modern capitalism are not possessed of a stronger acquisitive drive than, for example, an Oriental trader. The unleashing of pure greed has produced only irrational results; such men as Cortez and Pizarro, who were perhaps its strongest embodiment, were far from having an idea of a rationalistic economic life. As the economic impulse is universal, the interesting question is under which circumstances it becomes rationalised so as to produce rational institutions of capitalistic enterprise.

At the start two opposite attitudes towards the pursuit of

gain exist in combination. Inside the community there is attachment to tradition and pietistic relations with fellow members of tribe, clan and household which exclude unrestricted quest for gain within the circle of those bound together by religious ties; externally absolutely unrestricted pursuit of gain is permitted, as every foreigner is an enemy to whom no ethical considerations apply. Thus the ethics of internal and external relations are completely distinct. The course of development involves on the one hand the bringing of calculation into the relations of traditional brotherhood, displacing the old religious relationship . . . At the same time there is a tempering of the unrestricted quest for gain in relations with foreigners.

. . . The antipathy of Catholic ethics, and following that the Lutheran, towards every capitalistic tendency stems essentially from a repugnance towards the impersonality of human relations entailed by a capitalist economy, which places certain human actions beyond the influence of the church and prevents the latter from penetrating them and moulding them along ethical lines. The relations between the master and the slave could be regulated ethically, whereas it would be exceedingly difficult, if not impossible, to introduce moral considerations into the relations between the mortgage creditor and the property which was pledged for the debt, or between an endorser and the issuer of a bill of exchange. The consequence of the position adopted by the church was that medieval economic ethics excluded overpricing and free competition, and relied on the principle of just price to assure everyone of a chance to gain a livelihood.

The Jews cannot be made responsible for the breaking up of this circle of ideas. Their situation during the Middle Ages may be compared sociologically with that of an Indian caste in a world without other castes; they were an outcast people. However, the difference is that according to the promise of the Indian religion the caste system is valid for eternity. The individual may in the course of time reach heaven through a series of reincarnations, the length of time this takes depending upon his deserts; but this is possible only within the caste system. The caste organisation is eternal, and anyone who attempted to leave it would be accursed and condemned to pass in hell into the bowels of a dog. The Jewish religion, on the contrary, promises a reversal of caste relations in the future world. In the present world the Jews are branded as an outcast people, either as punishment for the sins of their fathers, as Deutero-Isaiah holds, or for the salvation of the world, which is the presupposition of the mission of Jesus of Nazareth; from which position they are to be released by a social revolution. In the Middle Ages the Jews were a guest people standing outside political society; they could not be received into citizenship because they could not participate in the communion of the Lord's Supper, and hence could not belong to the oath-bound fraternity.

The Jews were not the only guest people. The Caursines, for example, occupied a similar position. These were Christian merchants who dealt in money and in consequence were, like the Jews, under the protection of the princes, and on consideration of a payment enjoyed the privilege of carrying on monetary dealings. What distinguished the Jews in a striking way from the Christian guest peoples was the impossibility in their entering into convivial and matrimonial relations with the Christians. Originally the Christians did not hesitate to accept Jewish hospitality, in contrast to the Jews who feared that their ritual prescriptions about food would not be observed by their hosts. On the occasion of the first outbreak of medieval anti-semitism the faithful were warned by the synods not to conduct themselves unworthily and hence not to accept offerings from the Jews who on their side despised the hospitality of the Christians. Marriage with non-Jews was strictly excluded from the time of Ezra and Nehemiah.

A further ground for the outcast position of the Jews was the fact that agriculture could not be reconciled with the requirements of their ritual. Ritual considerations were responsible for the Jewish predilection for monetary dealings. Jewish piety demanded knowledge of the law and continuous study which were easier to combine with trade than with other occupations. Moreover, the prohibition of usury by the church entailed a condemnation of the exchange dealings indispensable to trade, and the Jews were not subject to ecclesiastical law.

Finally, Judaism had maintained the originally universal dualism of internal and external morality which allowed them to accept interest from foreigners who did not belong to the brotherhood or the community. This dualism legitimised other irrational types of business, especially tax farming and political financing of various kinds. In the course of the centuries the Jews acquired a special skill in these matters which made them useful and in demand. But all this was pariah capitalism, not rational capitalism such as developed in the West. Consequently, few Jews can be found among the creators of the modern economy, the large entrepreneurs; this type was Christian and only conceivable in Christendom. The Jewish manufacturer, in contrast, is a more recent phenomenon. The Jews could not have played a part in the establishment of rational capitalism because they were outside the craft organisations, even where, as in Poland, they had command over a numerous proletariat which they might have organised in the capacity of entrepreneurs in domestic industry or as manufacturers. Anyway, the Jewish ethic is traditionalist, as the Talmud shows. The pious Jew's horror of any innovation is as great as that of any primitive people steeped in magic.

Nevertheless, Judaism was of considerable importance for modern rational capitalism, in so far as it transmitted to Christianity its hostility towards magic. Apart from Judaism and Christianity, and two or three Oriental sects (one of which is in Japan), no religion is characterised by such a clear hostility towards magic. This hostility probably arose when the Israelites found in Canaan the magic of the agricultural god Baal, while Jahveh was a god of volcanoes, earthquakes and pestilences. The struggle between the two priesthoods and the victory of the priests of Jahveh discredited the fertility magic of the priests of Baal and stigmatised it as decadent and godless. Having made Christianity possible and given it the character of a religion essentially free from magic, Judaism played an important role in economic history, because the dominance of magic outside the Christian world constitutes one of the most serious obstacles to the rationalisation of economic life, as magic involves a stereotyping of technology and economic relations. When attempts were made to build railroads and factories in China a conflict with geomancy ensued, as the latter required that the location of structures on certain mountains, in forests, by rivers and on cemetery hills should not disturb the spirits' peace.*

Only great reforming and rationalising prophets could ever break the power of magic and establish a rational conduct of life . . . The prophets have released the world from magic and in doing so have created the basis for our modern science and technology, and for capitalism. No such prophets sprang up in China.

India, however, did produce a religion of salvation, and in contrast with China it has known great and prophetic missionary activities. But the typical Hindu prophet, such as Buddha, lives an exemplary life which leads to salvation, but does not regard himself as sent by God to insist upon everybody's obligation to follow his example, taking the position that whoever wishes for salvation can choose freely. Many may reject salvation, as it is not the destiny of everyone to enter at death into *nirvana*. Only philosophers imbued with hatred of this world are prepared to make the stoical resolution and withdraw from life.

The result was that Hindu prophets influenced only the intellectual classes who produced forest hermits and poor monks . . . Consequently Buddhism in its pure form was confined to a thin stratum of monks, while the laity found no ethical precepts according to which life should be led. True, Buddhism had its decalogue, but in distinction from that of the Jews it contained no binding commands, only recommendations. The most important good deed was to maintain the monks. Such a religious spirit could never displace magic, but only replace one kind by another.

In contrast to the ascetic religion of salvation of India and its weak influence on the masses, Judaism and Christianity

---

* A number of great scholars, such as John Mackinnon Robertson and James Frazer, take a different view of the relative place of magic in various religions. My own opinion on this matter is presented in two forthcoming books, *Max Weber's Errors and Greatness* and *Syphilis, Puritanism and Witchcraft*.

were from the beginning plebeian religions and have deliberately remained such. The struggle of the ancient church against the Gnostics was nothing else but a struggle against the aristocracy of the intellectuals, such as is common in ascetic religions, with the object of preventing their seizing the leadership in the church. This struggle was crucial for the success of Christianity among the masses, and hence for the fact that magic was suppressed among the general population to the greatest possible extent. True, it has not been extirpated even today, but it was degraded to the status of something unholy, and diabolic.

The germ of this change in the position of magic is found far back in ancient Jewish ethics, which is much concerned with matters which we also find treated in the proverbs and the so-called prophetic texts of the Egyptians. But the most important prescriptions of Egyptian ethics were futile because by laying a scarab on the region of the heart one could prepare a dead man to conceal successfully the sins he had committed, deceive the judge of the dead and thus enter into paradise. Jewish ethics knows no such sophisticated subterfuges and neither does Christianity. In the Eucharist the latter has indeed sublimated magic into the form of a sacrament, but it gave its adherents no means for evading the final judgement such as were provided by the Egyptian religion. To study the influence of a religion on life one must distinguish between its official teachings and the actual behaviour upon which in reality it places a premium in this world or the next.

We must also make a distinction between the religion of the adepts and the religion of the masses. Virtuoso religion affects everyday life only as an ideal; its claims are the highest, but they fail to determine everyday ethics. The relation between the two varies in different religions. In Catholicism they are brought into harmonious union in so far as the claims of the religious virtuoso are held up alongside the duties of the laymen as counsels of perfection. The truly perfect Christian is the monk; but his mode of life is not imposed on everyone, although some of his virtues in a modified form are held up as ideals. The advantage of this combination was that ethics was not split asunder as in

Buddhism, where the divergence between monastic ethics and mass ethics meant that the most worthy individuals in the religious sense withdrew from the world to establish a separate community.

Christianity was not alone in respect of this tendency, which recurs fairly frequently in the history of religions. The example of Tibet shows how enormous achievements can be made possible by an ascetically oriented methodical conduct of life. The country seems condemned by nature to be an eternal desert; but a community of celibate ascetics has carried out colossal construction works in Lhassa and moulded the country in accordance with the doctrines of Buddhism. In the Middle Ages in the West the monk is the first human being who lives rationally and works methodically and by rational means towards a goal, namely, the future life. Only for him did the clock strike, only for him were the hours of the day divided. The economic life of the monastic communities was also rational. The monks furnished a part of the officials during the early Middle Ages. The power of the doges of Venice collapsed when struggles about the investiture deprived them of the possibility of employing churchmen for overseas tasks.

However, the rational mode of life remained restricted to monastic circles. True, the Franciscan movement attempted to extend it to the laity through the institution of the tertiaries, but the institution of the confessional was a barrier to such an extension. The church domesticated the peoples of medieval Europe by means of its system of confession and penance. For the men of the Middle Ages the possibility of unburdening themselves through a confessional after they had rendered themselves liable to punishment meant a release from the consciousness of sin which the teachings of the church had instilled. The unity and strength of the methodical conduct of life were thus in fact broken up. In its knowledge of human nature the church did not rely on ethical consistency of the individual but steadfastly held to the view that in spite of the warnings of the confessional and of penances, no matter how severe, he would fall morally again and again. The church, therefore, shed its grace on the just as well as the unjust.

The Reformation made a decisive break with this system. The dropping of monastic ideals by the Lutheran Reformation meant the disappearance of the dualistic distinction between a universally binding morality and an especially demanding code for virtuosi. The other-worldly asceticism came to an end. The fervently religious individuals who would have gone into monasteries had now to practise their religion in ordinary life. Protestantism created an adequate ethic for such an asceticism within the world. Celibacy was not required provided that the pursuit of riches did not lead one astray into wanton enjoyment. Thus Sebastian Franck was correct in summing up the spirit of the Reformation when he said: 'You think you have escaped from the monastery, but now everyone must be a monk throughout his life.'

The tremendous significance of this transformation of the ascetic ideal can be still seen in the lands saturated by Protestant ascetic religiosity. The role of the religious denominations in America shows it vividly. Despite the separation of state and church, until fifteen or twenty years ago no banker or physician could take up a residence or establish connections without being asked to what religious community he belonged, and his prospects were good or bad according to his answer. Acceptance into a sect was preceded by a strict inquiry into one's ethical conduct. Membership of a sect which did not recognise the Jewish distinction between internal and external moral codes guaranteed one's business honour and reliability which in turn guaranteed success. This is the root of the principle 'honesty is the best policy' and of the ceaseless repetition among the Quakers, Baptists and Methodists of the saying based on experience that 'God would take care of his own'. 'The Godless cannot trust each other across the road; they turn to us when they want to do business; piety is the surest road to wealth.'

It is true that the accumulation of wealth, due to piety, led to a dilemma similar to that which the medieval monasteries repeatedly had to face: religious austerity led to wealth, wealth to fall from grace, and this again to the necessity of reconstruction. Calvinism sought to avoid this difficulty through the idea that man was only an administrator of what God had given him; it condemned enjoyment, yet permitted no flight from the world and regarded working with others under a rational discipline as the religious duty of the individual. Out of this system of ideas came our word 'vocation', which is known only to the languages influenced by the Protestant translations of the Bible. It expresses the value placed upon activity carried on according to the rational capitalist principle regarded as the fulfilment of a God-given task.* Here lay also the deepest roots of the contrast between the Puritans and the Stuarts, despite the fact that both were capitalistically minded. For the Puritan the Jew was likewise repugnant because he devoted himself to irrational and illegal occupations such as giving war loans, tax farming and leasing of offices, in the manner of the court favourite.

The idea of vocation gave to the modern entrepreneur a plentiful supply of industrious workers and crystal-clear conscience in exploiting them, while the latter were offered the prospect of eternal salvation as the reward of their ascetic devotion to work. In an age when ecclesiastical discipline controlled the whole of life to an extent inconceivable now, this idea had an impact quite different from any it might have today. Like the Catholic, the Lutheran churches recognised and practised ecclesiastical discipline. But in the Protestant ascetic communities admission to the Lord's Supper depended on ethical fitness which was identified with respectability in business, while no one inquired into the content of one's faith. Such a powerful, unconsciously refined organisation for the production of capitalistic individuals has never existed in any other church or religion, and in comparison with it what the Renaissance did for capitalism shrinks into insignificance. Its faithful occupied themselves with technical problems and were first-class experimenters. From art and mining, exper-

---

* It is symptomatic of the German tradition of dedication to work that the word *Beruf*, which Weber uses here, has no exact equivalent in English (nor in French, Spanish, or Polish). It can be translated, according to the context, as 'calling', 'vocation', 'occupation', 'employment', 'function', or 'profession'. Its moral loading stems from this width of meaning.

imentation was introduced into science. Although it did not transform the soul of man as did the innovations of the Reformation, the Renaissance view of the world exercised the main influence on the policy of rulers. Almost all the great scientific discoveries of the sixteenth century and even the beginning of the seventeenth were made in the environment of Catholicism. Copernicus was a Catholic, while Luther and Melanchthon condemned his discoveries. Scientific progress and Protestantism must not be unquestioningly identified. The Catholic Church has indeed on various occasions obstructed scientific progress; but the ascetic sects of Protestantism were equally inclined to have nothing to do with science, except in situations where material requirements of everyday life were involved. On the other hand it is Protestantism's specific contribution to have placed science in the service of technology and economics.

8
The Distinctive Features of European Cities and the Rise of the West

It is true that outside the Western world there were cities in the sense of a fortified point and the seat of political and ecclesiastic adminstration. But outside the Occident there were no cities in the sense of a unified community. In the European Middle Ages the distinguishing characteristic of a city was the possession of its own law and court and an autonomous administration. A man was a citizen in so far as he came under this law and participated in the choice of administrative officials. The absence of cities in the sense of a political community outside the Occident calls for explanation. It is doubtful whether the reason was economic. Nor does it seem that it was the 'Germanic spirit' which produced the unity; in China and India there were groups much more cohesive than those of the Occident, and yet the unified city is not found there.

The Occidental city arose through the establishment of a fraternity . . . The first example in the Middle Ages is the revolutionary movement in 726 which led to the secession of Italy from Byzantine rule and which centred in Venice. It was called forth especially by opposition to the destruction of holy images carried out by the emperors which means that religious dissent, although not the only factor, was the motive which precipitated the revolution. Until that time the dux (later doge) of Venice had been appointed by the emperor . . . From then on the choice of military leaders and of the ruler was in the hands of persons liable to military service as knights. Quite similar was the method of founding cities in Antiquity as, for example, the procedure of Nehemiah in Jerusalem. This leader induced the leading families and a selected portion of the people on the land to band themselves together under oath for the purpose of self-government and defence of the city. We must assume the same background for the origin of every ancient city. The *polis* is always the product of such a confraternity based on an oath of brotherhood . . . There are two reasons why this development took place only in the Occident. The first is the peculiar character of the organisation for defence. The Occidental city is in its beginnings primarily a defence group, an organisation of those economically competent to bear arms, to equip and train themselves.

Whether the military organisation is based on the principle of self-equipment or on that of equipment by a military overlord who furnishes horses, arms and provisions is a distinction quite as fundamental for social history as the question of whether the means of production are the property of the worker or of a capitalistic entrepreneur. Everywhere outside the West the development of the city was prevented by the fact that the army of the prince was older than the city. The earliest Chinese epics do not, like the Homeric, speak of the hero who fares forth to battle in his own chariot, but only of the officer as a leader of the men. Likewise in India an army led by officers marched out against Alexander the Great. In the West the army equipped by the ruler, and thus the separation of soldier from the tools of war (in a way analogous to the separation of the worker from the means of production), is a product of the modern era, while in Asia it stands at the outset of its historical development. There was no Egyptian or Babylonian-Assyrian army which would have presented a picture similar to that of the Homeric army, the feudal army of the West, the citizen army of the ancient city-state, or the medieval guild army.

The distinction is based on the fact that in the cultural evolution of Egypt, Western Asia, India and China irrigation was crucial. The question of water conditioned the existence of the bureaucracy, the compulsory service of the dependent classes and the dependence of the subject classes upon the bureaucracy of the king. That the king also extended his power in the form of a military monopoly is the fundamental difference between the military organisation of Asia and that of the West. In Asia the royal official and the army officer are from the beginning the central figures, while in the West both were originally absent. The forms of religious brotherhood and self-equipment for war made possible the emergence and existence of the city. The beginnings of an analogous development can be found in the East. In India we meet situations which verge upon the establishment of a city in the Western sense, namely, the combination of self-equipment and legal citizenship: a man in the free city of Vaicale who could furnish an elephant for the army is a full citizen. In ancient Mesopotamia, too, the knights waged war and established cities with autonomous administration. But in the one case as in the other these early 'cities' later disappear as the great kingdoms arise on the basis of water regulation.

The second obstacle to the development of the city in the Orient was formed by ideas and institutions connected with magic. In India the castes could not form ritualistic larger communities, and hence a city, because they were ceremonially segregated from one another. The same factor explained the peculiar position of the Jews in the Middle Ages. The cathedral and the Eucharist were the symbols of the unity of the city, but the Jews were not permitted to pray in the cathedral or take part in the communion and hence were doomed to form ghettos. On the contrary, the consideration which made it natural for cities to develop in Occidental Antiquity was its far-reaching freedom from the priesthood – the absence of any monopolisation by the priests of communion with the gods, such as obtained in Asia. In Greece and Rome the officials of the city performed the rites, and the city's ownership of things belonging to the gods and of the priests' treasures was carried to the point of filling the priestly offices by auction, since no magical limitations stood in the way as in India.

For the later period in the West three great facts were crucial. The first was the teaching of the prophets among the Jews, which destroyed magic within the confines of Judaism.

The second circumstance was the pentecostal miracle, the ceremonial adoption into the spirit of Christ which was a decisive factor in the extraordinary spread of the early Christian faith. The final turning point was the sermon in Antioch (Galatians 2: 11ff.) when Paul, in opposition to Peter, espoused fellowship with the uncircumcised. The magical barriers between clans, tribes and peoples, which were still known in the ancient city-state to a considerable degree, were thus set aside and the establishment of the Occidental city was made possible.

Although the city in the strict sense is specifically a Western institution, there are within the class two fundamental distinctions, first between Antiquity and the Middle Ages and secondly between southern and northern Europe. In the first period of development of the city communities the similarity between the ancient and medieval city is very great. In both cases it is those of noble birth who alone are active members in the group, while all the remaining population is merely bound to obedience. These knightly families become residents of the city for the sake of sharing in trade. After the success of the Italian revolution against Byzantium a group of Venetian upper-class families collected in the Rialto because from that point commerce with the Orient was carried on . . . In Antiquity there was no city of importance which lay more than a day's journey distant from the sea; only those places flourished which for political or geographical reasons possessed exceptional opportunities for trade. Consequently Sombart is essentially incorrect in asserting that ground rent is the fount of the city and of commerce. The facts stand in the reverse order; settlement in the city is occasioned by the possibility and the intention of employing the rents in trade, and the influence of trade on the founding of cities is decisive.

In the early Middle Ages the career of a successful individual in Venice was somewhat as follows. He began as a trader, that is, a retailer; then he proceeded to travel overseas, obtaining on credit from upper-class families money or goods which he turned over in the Levant, sharing his profit on his return with those who had provided the loan. If he was successful he could enter the Venetian higher circles by buying land or ships. As a shipowner or landowner he could ascend into the nobility until the closing of the Grand Council in 1297. The common designation of the members of the aristocracy living on the rent of land and of capital – both resting on trading profit – is 'honourable idler'. It is true that among the nobility in Venice there were always families which continued to carry on trade as a profession, just as in the period of the Reformation noble families who had lost their wealth turned to gaining a livelihood in industry. But normally the full citizen and member of an urban noble class is a man who possesses land as well as capital, and lives on an income but does not himself take part in trade or industry.

Thus far medieval development coincides with that of Antiquity; but their ways part with the establishment of democracy. At the outset, to be sure, there are similarities to be noted in this connection also: the noble is watched, deprived of the suffrage and outlawed, as the Russian bourgeoisie were by Lenin.

The basis of democratisation is everywhere purely military in character; it lies in the rise of disciplined infantry, the hoplites of Antiquity, the guild army in the Middle Ages. The decisive fact was that military discipline proved its superiority over the motley of heroes. Military discipline meant the triumph of democracy because the community wished, and was compelled, to secure the co-operation of the non-aristocratic masses and hence put arms, and along with arms political power, into their hands.

. . . The other method by which democracy established its domination was compulsory enrolment into the plebs. In Antiquity the nobles were forced to enrol in the tribes and in the Middle Ages in the guilds . . . Finally, there is everywhere a sudden and enormous multiplication of offices, a plethora of functionaries called forth by the need of the victorious party to remunerate its members with the spoils of the contest.

Thus far there is a parallel between the democracy of Antiquity and that of the Middle Ages. But alongside the points of agreement there are fundamental differences. At the outset there is the crucial distinction as regards the divisions into which the city falls. In the Middle Ages these consisted of the guilds, while in Antiquity they never possessed the guild character . . . We notice that guilds of different status successively rise to power. In Florence, the classical guild city, the earliest distinction was between the major crafts (*arti maggiori*) and the minor crafts (*arti minori*). The first group included, on the one hand, merchants, dealers in exchange, jewellers and other entrepreneurs who required a considerable industrial capital; and on the other, jurists, physicians, apothecaries and other 'persons of property and culture'. One may assume that in the guilds made up of entrepreneurs at least 50 per cent of the members lived on income from capital. This category of persons of property and culture was known as the *popolo grasso*, the 'fat' people. Exactly the same expression is found in the psalms, which are specifically the poetry of resentment of the virtuous and pious against the upper class of absentee owners and nobility, against the 'fat', as they are repeatedly called in the psalms themselves.

In the *arti maggiori* are included the small capitalists, while to the *arti minori* belong the butchers, bakers, weavers, and so on, who, in Italy at least, were on the fringe of the working class, although in Germany to some extent they became large entrepreneurs. The mere labourers, on the other hand, the *ciompi*, only exceptionally achieved power, as a rule only when the nobility allied itself with them against the middle class.

Under the rule of the guilds, the medieval city pursued a special policy. Its objective was in the first place to maintain traditional access to occupation and livelihood, and, secondly, to make the surrounding country subservient to the town through various obligations and compulsory use of the town market. It sought further to regulate competition and prevent the development of large-scale industry. In spite of this, an opposition developed between trading capital and craftsmen organised in guilds, in consequence of a growth of domestic industry and of a class of permanent journeymen, a forerunner of the modern proletariat. Nothing like this is to be found in Antiquity under the rule of democracy . . . In Antiquity the guild as the ruling power in the town is absent, and with it the economic privileges of the craftsmen as well as the opposition between labour and capital, such as can be found at the close of the Middle Ages.

In Antiquity we find in place of this conflict opposition between the landowners and the landless. The Roman proletarian is a disinherited descendant of a landowner and full citizen. The entire policy of the ancient city was directed towards preventing an increase in this class; to this end servitude for debt was restricted and the position of the debtor alleviated. The usual contrast in Antiquity was that between the urban creditor and the peasant debtor. In the city dwelt the money-lending patriciate; in the country, the small people to whom it lent its money; and under the ancient law of debt such a condition led readily to the loss of the land and proletarianisation.

. . . The opponents of the aristocracy in the Middle Ages were on the one hand the entrepreneurs and on the other the craft workers, while in Antiquity they were always the peasantry . . . The ancient city was divided along different lines from the medieval. In the latter noble families were compelled to join the guilds while in the ancient city they were forced into districts made up of rural landholders, in which they came under the same law as the peasants.

. . . The development of ancient democracies is characterised by the fact that the first to rise to power were the stratum of heavily armed footmen who were able to equip themselves with a coat of mail and a shield and who consequently could be employed in the front rank. Next, in consequence of the building-up of navies in some city-states, especially Athens, the non-possessing class rose to domination because the fleet could only be manned by including all strata of the population. The result of Athenian militarism was that in the popular assembly the sailors finally secured the whip hand.

. . . The typical citizen of the medieval guild city is a merchant or craftsman; he is a full citizen if he is also a householder. In Antiquity, on the contrary, the full citizen is a landholder. In the medieval city the non-landholder requires a landholder as his sponsor in order to acquire land; he is at a legal disadvantage, and this subordinate legal position is only gradually equalised and not everywhere completely. In his personal relations, however, the citizen of the medieval city is free. The principle 'town air makes free' asserted that after a year and a day a lord no longer had the right to recall his runaway serf . . . Hence the equalisation of classes and removal of unfreedom became a dominant tendency in the development of the medieval city.

In contrast the cities of Antiquity in the early period maintained the distinction between the patrician and the client, who followed the knightly warrior as a helper; they also recognised relations of dependency and slavery. But with the growth of the power of the city and its development towards democracy, the sharpness of class distinctions increased; slaves were imported in large numbers and formed a constantly growing lower stratum to which were added the freedmen. Hence the city of Antiquity, in contrast with that of the Middle Ages, showed increasing class inequality. Finally, no trace of the medieval guild monopoly is to be found in Antiquity. Even under Athenian democracy we find in the sources concerning the placing of the columns of the Erechtheion that free Athenians and slaves worked together in the same team and slaves were placed over free Athenian workers as foremen, which would have been unthinkable in the Middle Ages, in view of the existence of a powerful free industrial class.

. . . The democratic city of Antiquity was a political guild . . . Tribute, booty and the payments of confederate cities were widely distributed among the citizens. Like the craft guild of the late Middle Ages, the democratic citizens' guild of Antiquity was also interested in not admitting too many participants. The resulting limitation on the number of citizens was one of the causes of the downfall of the Greek city-states. The profits of this political guild included the distributing of conquered land and other spoils of war among the citizens; and payment out of the proceeds of this political activity for theatres, for allotments of grain, for jury service and for participation in religious rites.

Chronic war was therefore the normal condition of the Greek full citizen, and a demagogue like Cleon was conscious of his reasons for inciting to war; war made the city rich, while a long period of peace spelt ruin for the citizens. Those who engaged in the pursuit of profit by peaceful means were excluded from these opportunities for quick gains. They included the freedmen and resident foreigners among whom we first find something similar to the modern bourgeoisie, excluded from ownership of land but still well-to-do.

Military reasons explain why the city-state of Antiquity . . . developed no craft guilds, but instead achieved a political-military monopoly for the citizen and evolved into a warriors' guild. The ancient city represented the highest development of military technique in its time; no equivalent force could be sent against a hoplite army or a Roman legion. This explains the form and direction of economic endeavour in Antiquity in relation to profits from war, and other advantages to be attained by purely political means. On the other side from the citizen stands the 'low-bred' – anyone is low-bred who follows a peaceable quest for profit. In contrast, the centre of gravity of military technique in the early Middle Ages lay outside the cities, in the knighthood. No other force could equal a feudal host. The result was that the guild army of burghers – with the single exception of the Battle of Courtray in 1302 – never ventured offensive operations but was only defensively employed. Therefore the burgher army of the Middle Ages could never undertake the acquisitive function of the ancient hoplite or legion army.

Within the Western world we find during the Middle Ages a sharp contrast between the cities of the south and those of the north. In the south the nobility generally settled in the city, while in the north the opposite was the case; from the beginning they had their dwellings outside or were even excluded. In the north the grant of privileges to a city included the provision that it could prohibit the residence of high political officials or knights; on the other hand the knights of the north closed their ranks against the urban patriciate and treated the latter as inferior by birth. The cause of this difference was the fact that the founding of the cities took place in different epochs in the two regions. When the Italian communes began their rise the knightly military technique was at its height; hence the town was forced to take the knights into its pay or to ally itself with them. Therefore the townsmen insisted upon the knights taking up their residence in the city, as they did not wish them to operate from their castles to make the roads unsafe . . .

The most extreme contrast with these conditions is found in the English town which, in contrast to the German and Italian, never formed a city-state, and with rare exceptions was neither able nor sought to dominate the surrounding country or extend its jurisdiction over it. For this achievement it had neither the military power nor the desire. The independence of the English city rested on the fact that it leased fiscal authority from the king, and only those who shared in this lease, which designated a sum to be furnished by the city as a unit, were citizens. The special position of the English city is explained in the first place by the extraordinary concentration of political power in England after William the Conqueror, and further by the fact that after the thirteenth century the English communes were united in Parliament. If the barons wished to oppose the Crown, they were compelled to obtain financial aid from the towns, while the latter were dependent upon them for military support. From the time of their representation in Parliament the desire for (and the possibility of) a policy of isolation on the part of the towns was removed. The opposition between city and country soon disappeared and the cities accepted numerous landed gentlemen into their citizenship. The town burghers finally secured the upper hand, although until very recent times the nobility retained formal leadership in town affairs.

Turning to the question of the consequences of these factors for the evolution of capitalism, we must emphasise the multiplicity of non-rational forms of capitalism. These include, first, capitalistic enterprises involved in tax farming – in the Occident as well as in China and Western Asia – and in financing wars (in China and India, in the period of small separate states); secondly, capitalism connected with commercial speculation; thirdly, money-lending capitalism, exploiting the necessities of outsiders. All these forms of capitalism concern spoils, taxes, the pickings of office or official usury, exaction of tribute and preying on misery... Officials were financed as Caesar was by Crassus and endeavoured to recoup the sums advanced through misuse of their official position. All this, however, has the character of occasional economic activity of an irrational kind, while no rational system of labour organisation developed out of these arrangements.

Rational capitalism, in contrast, is organised with a view to market opportunities, that is, to economic objectives in the proper sense of the word, and the more rational it is the more closely it relates to mass demand and the provision for mass needs. It was modern Western development that elevated this capitalism into a system...

The capitalism of the late Middle Ages began to be directed towards market opportunities, while another contrast between it and the capitalism of Antiquity appears in the development after the cities lost their freedom... In Antiquity the freedom of the cities was swept away by a bureaucratically organised world empire within which there was no longer a place for political capitalism. In the beginning the emperors were forced to rely on the financial power of the capitalists, but progressively they emancipated themselves from such dependence and excluded this class from farming taxes and hence from the most lucrative source of wealth – just as the Egyptian kings were able to provide for political and military requirements in their realms independently of the capitalist class, and reduce the tax farmers to the position of tax officials. During the imperial period of Rome the leasing of public land everywhere decreased in extent in favour of permanent hereditary appropriation. Provision for the economic needs of the state was eventually made on the basis of compulsory contributions and labour instead of competitive contracts. The population became divided into classes along occupational lines and the burden of state requirements was imposed on the newly created groups on the principle of joint liability.

This development amounted to the throttling of ancient capitalism. A conscript army takes the place of the mercenaries and ships are provided by compulsory service.

The entire harvest of grain from the regions of surplus is distributed among the cities in accordance with their needs, with the exclusion of private trade. The building of roads and every other service which has to be provided for is laid on the shoulders of demarcated groups who become attached by hereditary bondage to the soil and to their occupations . . . After this system became established in the late Roman Empire as little room was left for capitalism as in the Egyptian kingdom of serfs.

Quite different was the fate of the city in the modern era. Here, again, autonomy was progressively taken away. English city government of the seventeenth and eighteenth centuries had ceased to be anything but a clique of guilds which could claim only financial and class privileges. German cities of the same period, with the exception of the imperial cities, became merely geographical entities in which everything was ordered from above. In French cities this development took place even earlier, while Spanish cities were deprived of their power by Charles V after the suppression of the insurrection of the *communeros*. Italian cities ended under the power of the princes, while those of Russia never achieved freedom in the Western sense. Everywhere military, judicial and industrial authority was taken away from the cities. Modern cities were deprived of their freedom as effectively as had happened in Antiquity with the establishment of Roman dominion; but in contrast to ancient cities, they came under the power of competing national states engaged in a perpetual struggle for power, whether in peace or war. This rivalry created the largest opportunities for modern Western capitalism. The separate states had to compete for mobile capital, which dictated to them the conditions under which it would assist them to augment their power. Out of this alliance of the state with capital, dictated by necessity, arose the national bourgeoisie in the modern sense of the word. Hence it was the national state that afforded capitalism its chance for development.

9
The State and Business Enterprise

The rational state has come into existence only in the Western world. Under the old regime in China a thin stratum of mandarins existed above the unbroken power of the clans and commercial and industrial guilds. The officials did not govern but only intervened in the event of disturbances or untoward happenings.

Very different is the rational state in which alone modern capitalism can flourish. Its basis is an expert officialdom and rational law . . . The rational law of the modern Occidental state, on the basis of which the trained official renders his decisions, evolved on its formal side, though not in its content, out of Roman law. The latter was originally a product of the Roman city-state, which never witnessed the dominion of democracy and its laws in the same form as the Greek city . . . Under Justinian the Byzantine bureaucracy brought order and system into this rational law, in consequence of the natural interest of the official in a law which would be systematic and fixed, and hence easier to learn.

After the fall of the Roman Empire in the West, jurisprudence was in the hands of the Italian notaries. These, and secondarily the universities, brought about the revival of Roman law. The notaries adhered to the old contractual forms of the Roman Empire and reinterpreted them according to the needs of the time. At the same time a systematic legal doctrine was elaborated in the universities. The essential feature in the development, however, was the rationalisation of procedure. As among all primitive peoples the ancient German legal trial was a rigidly formal affair. The party which pronounced wrongly a single word in the

THE STATE AND BUSINESS ENTERPRISE

formula lost the case, because the formula possessed magical significance and supernatural evils were feared . . . The magnificent administrative organisation of the church required fixed forms for its disciplinary ends in relation to the laity and for its own internal discipline . . . The businessman could not permit commercial claims to be decided by a competition in reciting formulas, and everywhere secured exemptions from this legalistic contest and from the ordeal. The church also, after hesitating at first, ended by adopting the view that such a procedure was heathenish and not to be tolerated, and established the canonical procedure on lines as rational as possible. This rationalisation of procedure . . . subsequently, spread over the Western world.

The revival of Roman law has been seen as the basis for the downfall of the peasant class, as well as for the development of capitalism. And it is true that there were cases in which the application of the principles of Roman law was disadvantageous to the peasant. An example is the transformation of the old community rights into feudal obligations, the individual who stood at the head of the community being recognised as a proprietor in the Roman sense and the holdings of the associates burdened with feudal dues. On the other hand, however, it was especially through the jurists trained in Roman law that in France the kings were able to obstruct the eviction of peasants by the lords.

Roman law was not an indispensable basis for the development of capitalism. England, the home of capitalism, never accepted Roman law, for the reason that in connection with the royal courts there existed a class of advocates who . . . determined the development of legal doctrine, for from its ranks were chosen, as they still are, the judges. It prevented the teaching of Roman law in English universities, to make sure that persons from outside its ranks could not reach the judicial bench.

In fact all the characteristic institutions of modern capitalism have origins other than Roman law. The annuity bond, whether arising out of a personal debt or a war loan, developed from medieval law, in which Germanic legal ideas played their part. Similarly the stock certificate had its origin in medieval and modern law and was unknown to the law of Antiquity. Likewise the development of the bill of exchange stems from Arabic, Italian, German and English laws. The commercial company is also a medieval product; only the *commenda* enterprise was known in Antiquity. Also the mortgage, with the security of registration, and the deed of trust, as well as the power of attorney, are medieval innovations and do not go back to Antiquity.

The reception of Roman law was crucial only in the sense that it created formal juristic thinking. In its structure every legal system is based either on formal-legalistic or on material principles. By material principles are to be understood utilitarian and economic considerations such as, for example, those according to which the Islamic cadi conducts his administration. In every theocracy and every absolutism justice is materially directed, as by contrast in every bureaucracy it is formal-legalistic. Frederick the Great hated jurists because they constantly applied in a formalistic sense his decrees which were based on material principles, and so turned them to ends of which he did not approve. In this connection, as in general, Roman law was the means of crushing the material legal system in favour of the formal.

Formalistic law is, above all, calculable. In China it may happen that a man who has sold a house to another may later come to him and ask to be taken in because in the meantime he has been impoverished. If the purchaser refuses to heed the ancient Chinese command to help a brother, the spirits will be disturbed; hence the impoverished seller comes into the house as a tenant who pays no rent. Capitalism cannot operate on the basis of a law so constituted. What it requires is law which can be counted upon, like a machine; ritualistic-religious and magical considerations must be excluded.

The creation of such a body of law was achieved through the alliance between the modern state and the jurists. In China, where the humanistically cultured mandarin ruled the field, the monarch had no jurists at his disposal, and the struggle among the different philosophical schools, as to which of them formed the best statesmen, swung to and fro

THE STATE AND BUSINESS ENTERPRISE

until finally orthodox Confucianism was victorious. India also had writers but no trained jurists. In contrast the Western world had at its disposal a formally organised legal system, the product of Roman genius, and officials trained in this law were superior to all others as technical administrators. The alliance between the state and formal jurisprudence was indirectly favourable to capitalism.

. . . An economic policy worthy of the name, that is, one which is continuous and consistent, is an institution of exclusively modern origin. The first such a policy was mercantilism . . . In the East essentially ritualistic considerations, including caste and clan organisations, prevented the development of a deliberate economic policy. In China the political system had undergone extraordinary changes. The country had an epoch of highly developed foreign trade, extending as far as India. Later, however, Chinese economic policy turned to isolationism, to the extent that the entire import and export business fell into the hands of only thirteen firms and was concentrated in the single port of Canton. At all times the question of ensuring co-operation between the provinces predominated, and a leading problem was the question of whether the needs of the state should be provided for by taxation or through compulsory services.

Japanese feudalism had the same consequences and resulted in Japan's complete isolation from the outer world. The object here was the stabilisation of class relations; it was feared that foreign trade would disturb the social relations and the distribution of property. In Korea ritualistic grounds determined the isolationist policy. If foreigners, that is, profane persons, were to come into the country the wrath of the spirits was to be feared. In the Indian Middle Ages we find records of the presence of Greek and Roman merchants, as well as Roman soldiers, and also the immigration of Jews with grants of privileges to them; but these germs were unable to develop, for later everything was again stereotyped by the caste system, which made a planned economic policy impossible. An additional consideration was that Hinduism strongly condemned travelling abroad; one who went abroad had on his return to be readmitted to his caste.

In the Occident until the fourteenth century a planned economic policy had a chance to develop only in the towns. It is true that there were beginnings of an economic policy on the part of the princes; in the Carolingian period we find attempts at price-fixing and various manifestations of concern for public welfare. But most of this remained on paper only, and with the exception of the coinage reform and the system of weights and measures of Charlemagne, everything disappeared without leaving a trace in the succeeding period . . .

The church interested itself in economic life, endeavouring to impose upon economic dealings a minimum standard of honesty and fairness. One of its most important measures was support of the public peace, which it attempted to enforce first on certain days and finally as a general principle. In addition, the great ecclesiastical communities, especially the monasteries, supported a very rational economic life, which cannot be called capitalistic economy but which was the most rational in existence.

The single measure of economic policy on the part of the German kings was the conflict over the Rhine tolls, which, however, was futile in the main, in view of the great number of petty lords along the river . . . The collection of customs was in the hands of the territorial princes, and even here with a few exceptions a consistent effort to encourage industry was lacking. Protective duties were unknown, with a few exceptions such as the duties on wine in Tyrol, directed against the competition of imports from Italy. The customs policy as a whole was dominated by the fiscal point of view and the aim of maintaining the traditional standard of living. The same applies to the customs treaties, which go back to the thirteenth century. The manner of levying customs fluctuated. The earliest custom was an *ad valorem* duty of one-sixtieth of the value; in the fourteenth century this was increased to a one-twelfth, in view of the fact that the duty was made to function also as an excise. Instead of our modern measures of economic policy, such as protective tariffs, there were direct prohibitions of trade, which were very frequently suspended when the standard of living of domestic craftsmen, or later of employing factors, was to be protected. Sometimes wholesale trade was allowed and retail trade was prohibited. The first trace of a rational economic policy on the part of the prince appears in the fourteenth century in England: mercantilism, as it has been called since Adam Smith's time.

The essence of mercantilism consists in carrying the point of view of capitalist industry into politics, as if the state consisted exclusively of capitalist entrepreneurs. External economic policy rests on the principle of taking every advantage of the foreigner, importing at the lowest price and selling much higher. The purpose is to strengthen the government in its external relations, by increasing the taxpaying power of the population ... The aim of mercantilist policy was the inclusion of as many sources of money income as possible within the country in question. The second point in the programme of mercantilism, obviously connected with power politics, was to promote the growth of the population: to provide for the increased numbers, the rulers endeavoured to extend external markets; especially for those products in which a maximum quantity of domestic labour was embodied, that is, finished manufactures rather than raw materials. Finally, trade was to be carried on as far as possible by the merchants of the country, in order that its earnings should augment the taxable capacity. These practices were justified by the doctrine of the balance of trade, which taught that the country would be impoverished if the value of imports exceeded that of exports. This theory was first developed in England in the sixteenth century.

England is the original home of mercantilism. The first traces of the application of mercantilist principles are found there in the year 1381. Under the weak King Richard II a shortage of money arose and Parliament appointed a commission which for the first time inquired into the balance of trade in all its essential aspects. For the time being it produced only emergency measures, including prohibitions of importation and stimulation of exportation, but without giving to English policy a truly mercantilist character. The real turning point is 1440. At that time, in one of the numerous Statutes of Employment which were passed for the correction of alleged abuses, two propositions were laid down which indeed had been applied before, but only in an incidental way. The first was that foreign merchants who brought goods to England must convert all the money they received into English goods; the second, that English merchants who had dealings abroad must bring back to England at least a part of their proceeds in cash. On the basis of these two principles there gradually developed the whole system of mercantilism down to the Navigation Act of 1651, with its prohibition of foreign shipping.

Mercantilism in the sense of an alliance between the state and capitalist interests had appeared under two aspects. One was that of class monopoly, which appears in its typical form in the policy of the Stuarts and the Anglican Church . . . However, in the sharpest possible contrast with Puritanism, which saw every poor person as work-shy or a criminal, its attitude towards the poor was friendly. In practice the mercantilism of the Stuarts had primarily fiscal aims: new industries were allowed only on the basis of a royal monopoly concession and were kept under the permanent control of the king with a view to fiscal exploitation. Similar, although not so consistent, was the policy of Colbert in France, who also aimed at an artificial promotion of industries, supported by monopolies.

. . . In England the royal and Anglican policy was broken down by the Puritans during the Long Parliament. Their struggle with the king was pursued for decades under the war cry 'down with the monopolies' which were granted in part to foreigners and in part to courtiers, while the colonies were placed in the hands of royal favourites. The small entrepreneur class which in the meantime had grown up, especially within the guilds though in part outside them, enlisted under this banner, and the Long Parliament deprived monopolists of the suffrage . . . Scarcely any of the industries created by mercantilism survived the mercantilist period; the economic creations of the Stuarts disappeared. It follows that capitalism was not an outgrowth of mercantilism, but developed at first in England alongside the fiscal monopolies . . . The class of entrepreneurs which had developed independently of the political administration

THE STATE AND BUSINESS ENTERPRISE

secured the systematic support of Parliament in the eighteenth century, after the collapse of the fiscal monopoly policy of the Stuarts. Here for the last time irrational and rational capitalism faced each other in conflict, that is, capitalism sustained by fiscal and colonial privileges and public monopolies against capitalism oriented to market opportunities for saleable commodities.

The point of collision of the two types was at the Bank of England. The bank was founded by Paterson, a Scottish capitalist adventurer of the type called forth by the Stuarts' policy of granting monopolies. But Puritan businessmen also had shares in the bank. The last time the bank turned in the direction of speculative capitalism was in connection with the South Sea Company. Aside from this venture we can trace step by step the process by which the influence of Paterson and his kind lost ground in favour of the rationalistic type of bank members who were all directly or indirectly of Puritan origin or influenced by Puritanism.

Mercantilism finally disappeared in England when free trade was established, an achievement of the Puritan dissenters Cobden and Bright, in league with industrial interests which were now in a position to dispense with support from the state.

157

10
The End of Capitalism?

The religious root of the modern economic outlook is dead; and the concept of a 'calling' is a relic in the world of today. Ascetic religiosity has been displaced by a pessimistic, though by no means ascetic, view of the world, as portrayed in Mandeville's *Fable of the Bees*, which teaches that private vices may under certain conditions lead to the good of the public. After the disappearance of the early religious fervour of the sects, the optimism of the Enlightenment which believed in the harmony of interests appeared as the heir of Protestant asceticism in the field of economic ideas, guiding the princes, statesmen, and writers of the later eighteenth and early nineteenth centuries. Economic ethics, which arose against the background of the ascetic ideal, has now been stripped of its religious support. The working class could accept its lot so long as the promise of eternal happiness was held out to it. When this consolation disappeared it was inevitable that society would begin to show the strains and stresses which have grown so rapidly since then. This point had been reached at the end of the early period of capitalism, at the beginning of the age of iron, in the nineteenth century . . .

Bureaucracy stifled private enterprise in Antiquity. There is nothing unusual in this, nothing peculiar to Antiquity. Every bureaucracy tends to intervene in economic matters with the same result. Whereas in Antiquity the policies of the city-state necessarily set the pace for capitalism, today capitalism itself sets the pace for bureaucratisation of the economy.

To have a true image of the later Roman Empire in modern terms, one must imagine a society in which the state

THE END OF CAPITALISM?

owns or controls and regulates the iron, coal and mining industries, all foundries, all production of liquor, sugar, tobacco, matches and all the mass consumption products now produced by cartels. In addition the state would have enormous domains, would run workshops to produce military supplies as well as goods for bureaucrats, would own all ships and railways, and would conclude state treaties to regulate wool imports. One must imagine the whole complex managed according to the rules of bureaucratic organisation, and along with it a system of guilds and a plethora of documents, academic or otherwise, needed for every activity. If we imagine all this, under a militaristic and dynastic regime, then we have summoned up the state of things under the later Roman Empire, the only difference being that the technological basis was not then so far advanced.

. . . Thus in all probability someday the bureaucratisation of society will encompass capitalism too, just as it did in Antiquity. We too will then enjoy the benefits of bureaucratic 'order' instead of the 'anarchy' of free enterprise, and this order will be essentially the same as that which characterised the Roman Empire and – even more – the New Empire in Egypt and the Ptolemaic state.

Index

administration 28; in Antiquity 51–6; in China 2, 60, 61, 76; in India 98–9
agriculture 39–40
Amerindian civilization 31
Ancient World, *see* Antiquity
annuity bonds 151–2
Antiquity 21, 26, 31; banking in 37; bureaucracy and 158; businessmen in 58; capital formation in 55–6; capital investment in 41–2; capitalist economy in 39, 56–8; cities in 60, 138, 140–6; citizens in 144–5, 148; city states 54–5, 58, 61, 144; corvée 36, 47; feudalism and 32–3; free labour 48–51; 'golden ages' of 41; government contracts 41; influence of politics 51; lack of factories 36–7; marine commerce 58; monarchies in 54–6; political theory in 57–8; precious metals in 42–3; public finance 51–6; slaves 34–6, 41, 43–51; tax-farming 10, 37, 47, 54–5; trade economy in 33–4; workers in 38; workshops in 46–7
architecture 22–3
armies 51, 98, 100, 139, 142, 148
art 22
Asia 59–60

Babylonia 21, 24–5, 32, 35, 42, 57, 61, 99, 139
Bank of England 157
banking 25, 37, 157
bill of exchange 152
bourgeoisie 27–8, 149
Brahmans 74, 88–9, 90, 93, 96, 101, 103–4, 105, 108
Bright, John 157
Buddhism 89, 132, 133–4
bureaucracy 1, 9, 158–9

capitalism 1, 3; birth in West 127; capitalist enterprise in Antiquity 42–56; church and 154; cities and evolution of 147–9; end of 158–9; entrepreneurs 122–3, 136; failure of development in Antiquity 56–8, 127; importance of law for 28; in Antiquity 39–42; in China 24–5, 73, 75–6; in Egypt 35–6; in late Middle Ages 148–9; institutions of 151–2; law and 152; pariah 131; population 126, 127; private 53–4; rational and irrational 8–9, 128, 131, 148; rational state and 150; slavery and 43–51; spirit of 111–18, 119, 122, 123, 125; textile industry and 120–1; traditionalism 117–18, 120–1; Western civilization and 24–9
Caursines 130
China 21, 29, 139; ancestral spirits 65, 77; bureaucracy in 71; capitalism in 24–5, 73, 75–6, 82–4, 126, 127, 147; 'castes' in 81; Chen Sui 69; cities in 60–2; clans 60, 62, 73, 77–9, 80; Confucians in 75; economy of 72–3, 80–4; emperor in 65, 66–7, 68–70, 71–2; Emperor Shih Huang Ti 67, 68, 71, 75; Emperor Yü 71; eunuch system 75; feudal nobility 68; forced labour 68–9; guilds in 60, 62–4, 73, 81; 'Homeric' age 66; imperial administration 2, 60, 61, 76; importance of education 74; irrigation in 64–5; law in 82–3, 152; Lu Pang 69; magic in 132; mandarins in 67–71, 74–5, 150; population 73, 126; public taxation 71; religion in 64–6; social structure of 80–4; sultanism 75; *Ta Ch'ing Lu Li* (Book of Laws) 83; trade in 60–1, 127, 153; unification of 67, 84; villages in 77; Wang An-Shih 74
Christianity 21, 129, 130–7; Calvinism 135–6; in America 135; Lutheranism 136, 137; monastic life 133–4; Puritanism 136; Reformation 135, 136
cities: as a defence group 139; bourgeoisie and 149; city states in Antiquity 54–5, 58, 61, 144; evolution of

capitalism and 147-9; feudal cities in Greece 32; guilds and 143-4, 146; in Antiquity 138-9, 140-6, 148; in China 60-2; in England 147, 149; in France 149; in Germany 147, 149; in Italy 146-7; in the Middle Ages 141-7; Jews and 140; lack of cities in the East 139-40; modern 149; of the north 146; of the south 146; religion and 140-1; rise of Western cities 138, 139, 140
Cobden, William 157
Colbert, Jean Baptiste 156
commercial company 152
Comte, Auguste 8
Copernicus, Nicholas 137

deed of trust 152
Descartes, René 8
duty 29

Eastern civilization 22-3, 25, 26, 30-2
economy: acquisition of money 114-15, 116-17, 124; capitalist economy in Antiquity 39, 56-8; German kings and 154; in China 72-3, 80-4; in the East 72; in the West 154-7; mercantilism 153, 155-7; religious roots of 158; trade 33-4; traditionalism and 128
Egypt 21, 24-5, 31, 32, 34, 42-3, 62, 64, 66, 139, 148, 149; bureaucratic order of 159; finance in 51-2, 72; grain storage 35; guilds in 91; labour in 35; religion 64, 78
England 147, 149, 155-7
ethics 127-8; Catholic 124, 129; Egyptian 133; Jewish 133; Protestant 1, 3, 115, 124-5, 129, 136

factories 36-7, 41
feudalism 5, 31-3, 153
Florence 125, 127, 143
Franklin, Benjamin 111-16, 119, 123, 124-5
free labour 35-6
Freud, Sigmund 7
Fugger, Jacob 113-14

Genoa 127
Greek civilization 3, 21, 51, 58, 74; agrarian systems 31; Athens 144; businessmen in 58; cities in 140; *ergastërion* 36, 46; feudal cities 32; finance in 52, 53, 57; precious metals in 43; slavery and 35, 36, 46; tax-farming 37; trade 33-4; war and 145

guilds 38, 60; in China 60, 62-4; in India 91-3, 100, 101; in the Middle Ages 143-4

Hinduism 86-91; Brahmans 74, 87, 88-9, 90, 93, 96, 101, 103, 105, 108; caste 90-1, 93-7, 104-8; dietary rules 95; 'guest peoples' 87-8; integration into 89

India 5, 21, 29, 34, 60, 66, 139; administration in 98-9; armies in 98, 100, 139; artisans in 106-7; Brahmans in 74, 87, 88-9, 90, 93, 96, 101, 103-4, 105, 108; Buddhism in 89, 100, 132; Buddhist monarchs in 83; bureaucracy 103-4; capitalism in 24-5, 126, 127, 147; caste in 90-1, 93-7, 104-8, 129-30, 140; census (1901) 96, 97; cities in 140; commerce 85; craftsmen in 101-3; economy in 106, 108; feudalism in 97; foreigners in 153; guilds in 91-3, 100, 101, 103; hereditary organisation 85; infanticide 95; Jainism in 89, 100; Jews in 85; Kshatriya 96; law in 22, 86; Mogul emperors 85; pariah peoples 88, 92; princes 100-1, 102, 103; sciences in 21-2, 28, 86; Shudra 96, 100; social system of 104-8; traditionalism of 108; unity in 85; urban development 86, 91, 99-100; use of money 99; Vaishya 96; villages in 85; Zarathustrians in 85; *see also* Hinduism
industrial civilization 9-10
Islam 21, 23, 72

Jainism 89
Jews/Judaism 65-6, 85, 129-31, 140, 153

Korea 153

Lecky, William 8
legal systems 10, 22, 28; canon law 151; formalistic law 152; German legal systems 150-1; in China 82-3; in England 151; Roman Law 150-3

INDEX

Luther, Martin 137

Machiavelli, Niccolo 22
magic 29, 131–2
Marx, Karl 106
Melanchthon, Philip 137
mercantilism 153, 155–7
Mesopotamia 64, 66, 140
Middle East 64
Mill, John Stuart 2
monastic life 133–4, 154
money-lenders 25
mortgage 152

officials 23

Parsons, Talcott 2, 5
Piraeus 33–4
population 126, 127
power of attorney 152
Puritanism 156, 157

rationality 7–10
Rhodes 34
religion 1, 3, 29, 64–5, 123, 131, 133–4, 154; *see also* ethics
Roman civilization 3, 51, 84, 149; agrarian systems 31; *annona* 35; bureaucracy and 158–9; cities in 140; city states 150; guilds in 91; precious metals and 43; private capitalists 53; proletarian 144; Roman law 150; slavery and 35–6, 45, 50; tax-farming 10, 37
Russia 35, 36, 37, 81

science 21–2, 28
slaves/slavery 34–6, 41, 42, 56; exploitation of labour 43–51, 57; female slaves 45; manumission 48–50; skilled slaves 47–8; slave agriculture 40; slave law 48
Smith, Adam 2
socialism 27
South Sea Company 157
Spain 127
Sparta 32
stock certificate 152
Stuarts, the 156–7

tax-farming 10, 37, 47, 52, 54–5, 147
Thucydides 22, 34
Tibet 134
Tocqueville, Alexis, Comte de 2

United States of America 116

Venice 127, 134, 138, 141–2

Weber, Max 1; career of 10–12; concept of rationality 7–10; *General Economic History* 4, 14; historical explanations 3–7; methodological writings 6; style of 2; *The Protestant Ethic and the Spirit of Capitalism* 3, 14; translations of 2–3; writings of 13–15, 16–17
Western civilization 1, 7; arts and 22–3; bourgeois class 27–8; capitalism and 24–9; development of settlements 30–1; economic policy in 154–7; feudal state 23–4, 31–3; law in 150–3; officials in 23; science and 21, 28

Lightning Source UK Ltd.
Milton Keynes UK
UKOW030326311012

201445UK00013B/64/P